How To Love The Rules of Golf

Howard J. Meditz
Applied Ink Press

Continued From Back Cover:

"Howard Meditz succeeds at demonstrating his infectious enthusiasm for golf and its Rules and understands the 'grasp' the game has on us. Will a read lead to a handicap drop — perhaps. Will you smile more during the round and become a better golf companion — very likely!"

Gene Westmoreland, Special Consultant, Metropolitan Golf Association; Former Member, numerous USGA National Championship Committees

"It's hard to find a resource that puts the Rules of Golf into a perspective that the average player can easily understand and the expert can readily benefit from as well. This book delivers exactly that. I love it!"

Kevin Carter, General Manager/Director of Golf, Turtleback Golf Course

"Howie shares a fun, clever and honest view of why he loves the Rules of Golf... and his love is contagious! His approach will improve the reader's decision making and lead to lower scores."

Rodrigo Valdés, Rules Official, National Rules Committee, Mexican Golf Federation

"Simply put, this book is an enjoyable read. Howard speaks to you through past experiences as he eloquently delivers the rules in a simplified manner. It never hurts to freshen up on your rules knowledge; and How to Love the Rules of Golf helps to explain the rules through popular mishaps and common misconceptions."

Mike Zamalkany, Manager, Championship Administration & Volunteer Operations, Metropolitan Golf Association

"How to Love the Rules of Golf is a great way to learn the rules of the game we all love to play. Being a PGA Golf Professional for 30 years, it really flummoxes me how many people lack knowledge of the rules. This book nails it — it's easy to understand and enjoyable to read. I will definitely be stocking it in our golf shop for members and guests. Great job Howie!"

Walter Janeczko, PGA Class A member, Certified US Kids Coach, TPI certified professional

I love Lisa.

The Rules of Golf too, sure, but mostly Lisa.

CONTENTS

A guide to where we've been, where we're going, enjoying the
game more when you're not playing your best, and being ecstatic
when you are
> Connect With Golf's History
> Score Better Under Pressure
> Get More Satisfaction From Every Round

A comprehensive review of the extraordinary Rules education
opportunities available — the majority of which are absolutely free

Golf's equivalent to relationship counseling
> "That's Such A Stupid Rule!"
> "The Rules Of Golf Are Hopelessly Outdated."
> "The Rules Are Way Too Complicated."
> Stroke And Distance Penalty
> Relief From A Fairway Divot Hole
> Repair Of Spike Marks On The Green
> Requirement To Take Full Relief
> Tree Roots, Stones, Hardpan And Rubs Of The Green

An introduction as to how the USGA and R&A think the Rules
might change, the value of those changes, and how you can
participate in shaping them

⚐ ⚐ ⚐

INTRODUCTION

So what's all this about loving the Rules of Golf?

My high school golf coach's real job was coaching our football team, but off-season he worked with the golf team. He was crazy about the game, didn't let the fact that he could barely break 100 stop him from "teaching" us, and as a bonus brought some football flair with him to the course: "Meditz, if you can't win by playing fair, don't lose!"

Coach Coady was kidding with that admonition, but it focused me. Sure, I was proud of myself when I won — but I discovered that I was also proud when I lost since unlike some of my adolescent competitors I tried to follow all the Rules of Golf all the time as the "Spirit of the Game" demands.

Feel good when you win *and* when you lose? I'm sold!

Following the Rules is a simple but profound choice. To this day every time I see someone call a penalty on himself that he could just as easily have hidden, my inner voice whispers, "Yes, I completely understand, respect and appreciate that bittersweet feeling."

You can't beat golf. But you can stand up to it.

⚐

I study and debate the Rules almost every day with people around the world. That ritual combined with years of academic training, field training and officiating experience has given me the opportunity to witness the impact the Rules have in a vast number of situations. I'm continually amazed at how beautifully the Rules are woven together and, when you look at them very closely, how uncompromisingly fair they are. (Having an appreciation of how that "fairness" works not only makes the Rules easier to remember, but perhaps more important, it makes the Rules easier to stomach during, shall I say, our more "difficult" moments.)

I'm fully aware that not everyone shares my affection for this grand matrix of words. But I also know that when I offer my perspective on a Rule to people I'm chatting with, or randomly grouped with when I'm playing, or even officiating for when I'm working — I can often turn them around. That's exactly what I hope to do through this book, to inspire you to fully embrace the Rules and to show you how truly satisfying that can be.

In fact, if you let them, the Rules of Golf can be your personal path toward golf happiness — irrespective of your playing ability.

That's truly something to love.

I. HOW TO EMBRACE THE RULES OF GOLF

Since you'll want to be properly introduced before you even consider falling in love, that's where we'll start.

Golf is a worldwide game, and the Rules of Golf are jointly issued by the United States Golf Association headquartered in Far Hills, New Jersey (which has governance for the United States and Mexico) and the St Andrews, Scotland-based R&A Rules Limited (which administers these same Rules for the rest of the world). Together they're often referred to as the "Ruling Bodies."

Today's Rules are incredibly refined. The way they provide specific guidance for every imaginable situation — and even for situations which haven't yet been imagined — is downright fascinating.

It's really gratifying to get better at golf, but the sport is so quirky, courses are so different, and most every player's day-to-day performance is so erratic that it's hard to tell how much you're improving. Fortunately, for more than 270 years some very devoted people have been analyzing, advancing and formalizing a precise and comprehensive way to judge your progress: The Rules of Golf.

Sometimes people find the Rules hard to accept. They get frustrated when they're called out on a silly mistake — a mistake which might not have even given them an advantage. But there's an alternative perspective on this, and those open to it will discover there can be immense satisfaction hidden within all the rigors and technicalities of the Rules of Golf.

There are lots of different routes we can take to approach the Rules in this optimistic way, and we're going to take them all.

Connect With Golf's History

There are two things I think about on the first tee every time I play. Number one: "This has a chance to be the best round of my life." Number two: "People just like me have been trying to measure up to the demands of this game for more than 500 years." I really like both of those ideas. They're true and they put me in a great frame of mind. (The second of the two is particularly appealing since it never disappoints.) There's a lot to appreciate about the traditions in golf. The R&A's Open Championship dates back to 1860, and the USGA's U.S. Open has been played since 1895. Perhaps even more impressive is the fact that the very beginnings of the Rules themselves have been preserved. The first known effort is more than a century older than even the Open Championship! Part of my appreciation for the Rules comes from the fact that they've been honored by so many people for such a long time. It's awesome that we can join with these people by tracing the basic Rules back to their origins and by playing much the same game today as they did then.

Ɓ

As early as the 1500s, Leith Links was a five-hole golf course in an area that is now part of Edinburgh, Scotland. On March 7th, 1744, the Gentlemen Golfers of Leith (a group later to become Muirfield's Honourable Company of Edinburgh Golfers) created the first written Rules of Golf. The group had petitioned the Edinburgh Council to provide it with a Silver Club as a trophy for its upcoming April 2nd tournament, "an annual competition among Noblemen and Gentlemen from any part of Great Britain and Ireland." As a condition of its cooperation, the Council required that formal Rules first be established, and so they were. And some 270 years later, here they are:

ꝓ ꝓ ꝓ

Articles & Laws in Playing at Golf.

1. You must Tee your Ball within a Club's length of the Hole.
2. Your Tee must be upon the Ground.
3. You are not to change the Ball which you Strike off the Tee.
4. You are not to remove Stones, Bones or any Break Club, for the sake of playing your Ball, Except upon the fair Green & that only within a Club's length of your Ball.
5. If your Ball comes among watter, or any wattery filth, you are at liberty to take out your Ball & bringing it behind the hazard and Teeing it, you may play it with any Club and allow your Adversary a Stroke for so getting out your Ball.
6. If your Balls be found any where touching one another, You are to lift the first Ball, till you play the last.
7. At Holling, you are to play your Ball honestly for the Hole, and not to play upon your Adversary's Ball, not lying in your way to the Hole.
8. If you shou'd lose your Ball, by it's being taken up, or any other way, you are to go back to the Spot, where you struck last, & drop another Ball, And allow your adversary a Stroke for the misfortune.
9. No man at Holling his Ball, is to be allowed, to mark his way to the Hole with his Club, or anything else.
10. If a Ball be stopp'd by any Person, Horse, Dog or anything else, The Ball so stop'd must be play'd where it lyes.
11. If you draw your Club in Order to Strike, & proceed so far in the Stroke as to be bringing down your Club; If then, your Club shall break, in any way, it is to be Accounted a Stroke.
12. He whose Ball lyes farthest from the Hole is obliged to play first.
13. Neither Trench, Ditch or Dyke, made for the preservation of the Links, nor the Scholar's Holes, or the Soldier's Lines, Shall be accounted a Hazard; But the Ball is to be taken out, Teed and play'd with any Iron Club.

John Rattray, Capt

Local surgeon John Rattray ("Captain of the Golf") signed the Rules for "Playing at Golf," and went on to win that year's contest as well as others in following years. Ten years later, these Leith Links Rules were almost entirely adopted by a group which eventually became known as The Royal and Ancient Golf Club of St Andrews for its first competition, held on May 14, 1754.

HOW TO LOVE THE RULES OF GOLF | 5

It should surprise no one who has ever played this game that some people found frustration with the established Rules. Back at Leith, a subsequent Captain of the Golf (I love that title!), Thomas Boswall, attested to this in 1758 when he issued the following update to the 1744 Rules:

Amendment to the Articles & Laws - 1758

The 5th, and 13th Articles of the foregoing Laws having occasioned frequent Disputes It is found Convenient That in all time Coming, the Law Shall be, That in no Case Whatever a Ball Shall be Lifted without losing a Stroke Except it is in the Scholars holes When it may be taken out teed and played with any Iron Club without losing a Stroke - And in all other Cases the Ball must be Played where it lyes Except it is at least half Covered with Water or filth When it may, if the Player Chuses be taken out Teed and Played with any Club upon Loosing a Stroke.

Thomas Boswall, Capt

Captain Boswall's efforts to improve upon the Rules were no doubt sincere, but I think we can all agree that his phrase, "That in all time Coming" was a bit too optimistic. You've probably noted there have been further changes to the 13 original Rules leading us to the 34 Rules by which we play today. (Irrespective of the obvious value of all the changes since 1758, I want to go on record as wishing we still called Water Hazards, "Wattery filth." It feels right.)

The R&A remained dedicated to playing by and improving these Rules over the next 130 years or so, and the United States Golf Association decided to join in on both fronts when it was officially formed in New York City on December 22, 1894 under its initial name, the Amateur Golf Association of the United States. Over time the USGA developed Rules which were somewhat different from the R&A's, and noteworthy distinctions would exist for almost 100 years afterwards. In fact, while the USGA and R&A finally got together and agreed to jointly issue uniform Rules and updates to the Rules of Golf starting January 1, 1952, the ongoing "uniformity" of the Rules still suffered fits and starts over the next 38 years.

At times the minimum diameter of the ball had different specifications issued by the two Ruling Bodies, at times there were differences regarding the application of the Stroke and Distance penalty, and in fact while the main Rules themselves remained closely parallel since 1952, the complex and important Decisions on the Rules were still not uniform until 1984 (after the culmination of a nine year effort to resolve differences). Ultimately, it wasn't until 1990 that both organizations at last agreed to what is the final standardization of the minimum diameter of the golf ball at 1.68 inches. So today, with the exception of essentially irrelevant distinctions such as the spelling of the word "honor" (or "honour") when referring to who tees off first in Rule 10-1a, or using dollars (or pounds) to describe the value of prize limits in the Rules of Amateur Status section, we players finally have a single set of worldwide Rules upon which to rely.

It's nice to see that for the first time the cover of the 2016 *Rules of Golf* sports both the R&A's and the USGA's logos side by side. I suspect John Rattray, the Captain of the Golf and noteworthy member of the Gentlemen Golfers of Leith would be pleased. Much has been accomplished in the preceding 272 years, and we get to appreciate it. The history of our Rules continues to unfold though, so keeping abreast of improvements is part of our challenge. For me, seeing how our sport advances in this way is also part of the fun of being connected to golf.

⚑

Score Better Under Pressure

Playing well under pressure is one of the most exciting rewards in golf. And here's a truth: being accustomed to playing strictly by the Rules can significantly limit anxiety and frustration during formal competitions.

We've all seen the guy who misses a two-foot down-hill putt for par in casual play and then rakes away the resulting four-footer, quietly grumbling as he puts himself down for a bogey. Let's call him "Joe." His buddies think nothing of it, they do the same thing — it's kind of an unwritten rule in their friendly group. But two weeks later, Joe is playing in a Stroke Play tournament. He misses the same two-footer, then lips out the return putt and has to tap in for a double. Adrenaline pumps out of his ears. He can't believe this! Nobody three-putts from two feet!

Joe, I respect your right to play golf any way you wish, but you're absolutely wrong about this. People *do* three-putt from two feet. Sometimes even pros do.

If Joe changed his habit after missing a short putt to assessing and stroking the return, he'd learn that he will occasionally miss that subsequent four-footer. And he'd emotionally adjust to the unfortunate fact that golf doesn't give a damn that he just missed a two-footer, it only cares whether he makes the resulting four-footer. (Golf knows well that a four-footer is not a gimme — for either pros or amateurs.) So my friend Joe here has traded a simple "Darn, I missed that one" for an emotional "I suck at golf!" And maybe a club toss. He then ends up spending the next three holes compounding his mistake because he can't get the "injustice" (embarrassment) of that three-putt out of his mind.

(It's worth pointing out here that I'm not advocating slow play. We all share an important obligation to keep pace, and we all should consistently do just that. But I am saying that everyone who is reasonably capable of playing Stroke Play golf doesn't need to give themselves putts in order to keep up. There are lots of ways to improve your pace. Opinion: If you don't have time to putt a four-footer, you don't have time to play golf.)

Back to Joe, not holing out in regular Stroke Play is just one way that his customarily liberal approach to the Rules hurts him in tournaments. Let's look at another. Joe's drive ends up in a good lie in the rough, but his feet are on a paved cart path. On his typical Saturday he would pick his ball up and toss it left into a nice grassy area without thinking anything of it. But today Joe is playing in a tournament. He picks his ball up from near the cart path and his Fellow Competitor wanders over to watch.

Joe knows he has to drop within one club-length (no closer to the hole) of the Nearest Point of Relief, but he didn't realize when he lifted his ball that in this particular case the nearest point isn't left of the path in that pleasant area where he's used to tossing his ball, the Nearest Point of Relief for the ball and Joe's stance is actually on the right side of the path. And there's nothing but rocks over there on the right! What now? I think you know... Joe traded in his initial acceptable lie (that had a little irritation regarding his stance) for a really ugly lie on rocks, a resulting terrible shot, and three more holes of desperately trying to calm himself down. "Oh man" Joe thinks, "I'm having the worst luck today."

Ƿ Ƿ Ƿ

No Joe, you're playing golf. Play by the Rules all the time and you'll easily get used to it. You'll enjoy your tournaments more and score better in them by virtue of minimizing your frustration — because in future tournaments you'll be playing the exact same game you're used to playing every Saturday.

Ƿ

I could go on and tell you how Joe felt in front of the crowd on the eighteenth hole when he realized he scooped up his ball from the lip of the cup with the back of his putter instead of tapping it in, but I won't.

Ƿ

In addition to the fact that regularly playing strictly by the Rules enhances tournament performance by reducing frustration, there's the parallel fact that it's confidence-building to know how to approach any Rules situation that's likely to come up. The best pros will tell you that golf is a game of confidence, and carrying the assurance that you know what you're doing in the Rules realm doesn't just help you avoid costly mental mistakes. When you factor in the impact on your confidence in general, it can even indirectly help you swing the club.

Ƿ

Get More Satisfaction From Every Round

At its heart, golf is a confounding game. You can successfully make a particular shot dozens of times, and then for no apparent reason flub it the next time you try. With that kind of frustration lurking around every green, it's not surprising that the idea of adding a two-stroke penalty for, say, accidentally touching the sand with your club while your ball is in a bunker can be seen as an unappealing choice. As a result, as I alluded to at the beginning of this chapter, some people are reluctant to play the game by all of its Rules, and habitually ignore the ones that bother them the most.

But here's another truth: in the long run, making arbitrary choices to avoid the consequences of some of the Rules takes much more away from you than it gives. Taking liberties ends up preventing you from knowing how well you really played, and consequently prevents you from knowing how good you really are. Ultimately, taking liberties stands in the way of enjoying golf to the fullest.

Said another way, if you are humble enough to accept how good you are when you play strictly by the Rules, you can thoroughly enjoy all of your legitimate accomplishments from that time forward. I'm not an impressive player, I've broken 80 a grand total of two times in my life. But I can tell you that the satisfaction I take in my 79 and my 78 far surpasses the pleasure I'd feel if I had fluffed a lie on either of those momentous days. That feeling of unadulterated pride is something available to everyone who is willing to reach for it.

If you don't already, I sincerely recommend that you do exactly that: Reach for it. If you've been playing by a softer, self-modified, less objective set of rules you'll undoubtedly have a period of adjustment — it's likely that what you think you typically shoot isn't as low a score as what the Rules of Golf reveal. But once you adjust to the truth, you'll be ready for anything.

However you play, I predict that driving home knowing what you actually scored will be far more fulfilling than driving home having a debate with yourself about what you would have scored if you hadn't taken that mulligan on the sixth.

⚐

There are two other critical aspects related to embracing the Rules: believing that they'll be fair to you, and appreciating the scoring benefits you'll get when you really know how to use the Rules to your advantage. In fact, each of these two issues is so important that it's "new chapter worthy." After we cover how to get to know the Rules better, we'll get back to those key topics.

Whenever practical, when a concept related to a Rule, Local Rule, Decision, or Definition from the Rules of Golf is being discussed the precise wording from the Rule will be presented under three "floral hearts" on the preceding page (or pages) so you can conveniently review the details. Note that italicized words in these segments indicate that those words have a specific "golf Definition" provided within the Definitions section of the Rules.

❧ ❧ ❧

Rule:

6-1. Rules
The player and his *caddie* are responsible for knowing the *Rules*. During a *stipulated round*, for any breach of a *Rule* by his *caddie*, the player incurs the applicable penalty.

Definition:

Rule or Rules
The term "*Rule*" includes:
a. The Rules of Golf and their interpretations as contained in "Decisions on the Rules of Golf";
b. Any Conditions of Competition established by the *Committee* under Rule 33-1 and Appendix I;
c. Any Local Rules established by the *Committee* under Rule 33-8a and Appendix I; and
d. The specifications on:
   i. clubs and the ball in Appendices II and III and their interpretations as contained in "A Guide to the Rules on Clubs and Balls"; and
   ii. devices and other equipment in Appendix IV.

⚑ ⚑ ⚑

II. HOW TO GET TO KNOW THE RULES

Learning the Rules of Golf can be a lot of fun, and certainly doesn't have to be a grueling marathon. It's much better approached a little at a time as you would a hobby — one you can enjoy more and more as time goes on. I live in the United States, and I'm a member of the USGA, so my suggestions on how to educate yourself on the Rules come from my experience here. There are various parallels provided for people who reside elsewhere, most notably by the St Andrews-based R&A.

⚑

Rule 6-1: The Player And His Caddie Are Responsible For Knowing The Rules.

I don't care what anyone tells you. The Rules of Golf are not simple. There are nominally "just" 34 Rules, but many of those 34 have significant subsets (for instance Rule 25 covers the three somewhat dissimilar topics of Abnormal Ground Conditions, Embedded Ball and Wrong Putting Green). Add to that the 50 or so Definitions (each of which has the status of a Rule), the more than 1,200 Decisions on the Rules of Golf (again, each having the status of a Rule and collectively so vast as to require a separate book), optional Local Rules and possible Conditions of Competition and it's easy to see that complying with Rule 6-1 puts quite a bit on your plate.

There are many books which endeavor to explain the Rules of Golf. You might very well get things of value from them, but here's a thing of beauty: much of the collective wisdom of the USGA's and R&A's hundreds of years of Rules knowledge is available to you directly, and absolutely free. You can go to www.USGA.org (or alternately www.RandA.org) and you'll not only have free access to the *Rules of Golf*, but also to the broader *Decisions on the Rules of Golf* as well as a plethora of other engaging free resources. (If you like, for a modest fee you can get the USGA's smartphone app putting the Rule book and the extensive Decisions book conveniently on your phone.)

⚑ ⚑ ⚑

While I'm busy shamelessly promoting the USGA's efforts, let me add that as of this writing the USGA offers the best deal in all of golf: when you become a member, for a mere $10.00 you get a hard copy of the *Rules of Golf*, a U.S. Open golf hat, your name inscribed on a USGA bag tag, and some other benefits — shipping included. I don't know about you, but to me that's an amazing bargain. (If you just want a hard copy of the *Rules of Golf*, the USGA website actually "sells" it for free — you just pay for shipping and handling.)

⚑

If you don't already have a hard copy of the *Rules of Golf* there are two different ways to view the Rules on the USGA's website: There's a PDF of the complete book, and there's an interactive version containing the main body of the *Rules of Golf* mixed with the *Decisions on the Rules of Golf*. If you want to see the PDF of the whole book, type "2016 USGA Rules of Golf" into the search function symbol accessed from the top right of the USGA home page. Viewing the whole book gives you the advantage of being able to read the instructional segments presented prior to the Rules themselves as well as the "Rules of Amateur Status" and "Policy on Gambling" toward the end, and lastly the very useful index at the very end of the book. If you instead click on "Rules" on the top of the homepage and then "Rules & Decisions," you won't get these "book-only" features but instead you'll get both the Decisions and Rules interactively woven together — along with the ability to click yourself directly to a Definition, alternate Rule or related Decision whenever you choose. Each approach has its advantages.

⚑

While there is no shortage of free information about the Rules, it can be surprisingly hard to figure out the best way to get started. My suggestion is to start at the source by grabbing a copy of the *Rules of Golf* and begin by reading the Definitions section near the beginning. The Definitions are critical. You have to know exactly what's meant by the specific words and phrases defined in the book or you'll quickly get lost when you try to accurately apply the Rules to your game.

For instance, even the fundamental Definition of a golf "Stroke" is more specialized than what you might assume from the ordinary English language definition of the word (e.g., your backswing isn't part of your stroke — from a Rules perspective your backswing is a separate endeavor).

After you peruse the Definitions, check out the two-page "How to Use the Rule Book" section in the hard copy or PDF and then the eight-page "A Quick Guide to the Rules of Golf" segment at the beginning. Those ten pages do a really nice, concise job of getting you going. Don't be intimidated by the scope of all of this, **reading just those brief sections at the beginning of the *Rules of Golf* will get you pretty far along in your quest for knowledge** — *in my experience much further along than many skilled players who mistakenly think they know the Rules but have missed some of the finer points in that ten-page summary.* (I'm sorry to say I mean that quite literally. The number of experienced players I talk to who hold slight misunderstandings regarding the common practices of taking relief from Obstructions, Water Hazards and Abnormal Ground Conditions is very surprising — particularly given the fact that these issues are so well covered in the eight Quick Guide pages.)

Even if you don't want to sit down to read the entire *Rules of Golf* right away, if you read the two sections I noted and then the titles of the 34 Rules (listed on page 3 and 4 in the table of contents), you'll have an excellent idea of what to do in most situations. Or at least you'll know where to look further when you come across an unresolved problem.

Definition:

Holed

A ball is *"holed"* when it is at rest within the circumference of the *hole* and all of it is below the level of the lip of the *hole*.

Rule:

17-4. Ball Resting Against Flagstick

When a player's ball rests against the *flagstick* in the *hole* and the ball is not *holed*, the player or another person authorized by him may move or remove the *flagstick*, and if the ball falls into the *hole*, the player is deemed to have *holed* out with his last *stroke*; otherwise, the ball, if *moved*, must be placed on the lip of the *hole*, without penalty.

⚑ ⚑ ⚑

The physically small size of the Rule book is no accident. It (or the equivalent smartphone app) easily fits in your golf bag for good reason. Say your ball gets stuck between a leaning flagstick and the edge of the hole, stopping slightly above the lip. Is it holed? Pull out the book and look at the Definition of "Holed" and you'll find that it isn't. Now what? Look at Rule 17 (The Flagstick), scan to 17-4 (Ball Resting Against Flagstick), and all is revealed. And if which Rule to read isn't obvious in a given situation, the extensive index at the back of the book can help you find your answer relatively quickly.

My next step for those who are willing to put a little more effort into becoming their regular group's Rules Guru is to read the entirety of Rule 20 (Lifting, Dropping and Placing; Playing from Wrong Place) since at least one of those actions comes up almost every hole.

Then you'll want to access the Decisions, either online as described above or by purchasing a hard copy of *Decisions on the Rules of Golf*. Reading Decision 26-1/1 (Meaning of "Known or Virtually Certain") is quite important since it has application to getting possible relief from so many different conditions (Water Hazard relief, free relief from Obstructions and Abnormal Ground Conditions, and in some instances free relief if your ball was moved or even stolen by someone). Next, back to the main book (or snapping back and forth interactively), reading the entirety of Rule 26 Water Hazards will serve you well.

⚑

It might be useful for you to note that "Rules" are labeled with numbers and dashes and letters such as: Rule 26-1 or Rule 26-1a. "Decisions" are labeled with numbers and dashes and letters too, but they always have a slash as well such as Decision 26/1 or the aforementioned 26-1/1. (Those are two separate Decisions, the first a Decision related to "Rule 26: Water Hazards" in general, the second a Decision specifically related to the subset "Rule 26-1: Relief for Ball in Water Hazard." The general Decisions on a Rule always precede the more specific subset's Decisions in the book.)

☙ ☙ ☙

Definitions:

Obstructions
An "*obstruction*" is anything artificial, including the artificial surfaces and sides of roads and paths and manufactured ice, except:

a. Objects defining *out of bounds*, such as walls, fences, stakes and railings;
b. Any part of an immovable artificial object that is *out of bounds*; and
c. Any construction declared by the *Committee* to be an integral part of the *course*.

An *obstruction* is a movable *obstruction* if it may be moved without unreasonable effort, without unduly delaying play and without causing damage. Otherwise, it is an immovable *obstruction*.

Note: The *Committee* may make a Local Rule declaring a movable *obstruction* to be an immovable *obstruction*.

Loose Impediments
"*Loose impediments*" are natural objects, including:

*   stones, leaves, twigs, branches and the like,
*   dung, and
*   worms, insects and the like, and the casts and heaps made by them, provided they are not:
    *   fixed or growing,
    *   solidly embedded, or
    *   adhering to the ball.

Sand and loose soil are *loose impediments* on the *putting green*, but not elsewhere.

Snow and natural ice, other than frost, are either *casual water* or *loose impediments*, at the option of the player.

Dew and frost are not *loose impediments*.

Decision:

23/3 Half-Eaten Pear
Q. A half-eaten pear lies directly in front of a ball in a bunker and there is no pear tree in the vicinity of the bunker. In the circumstances, is the pear an obstruction rather than a loose impediment, in which case the player could remove it without penalty?

A. No. A pear is a natural object. When detached from a tree it is a loose impediment. The fact that a pear has been half-eaten and there is no pear tree in the vicinity does not alter the status of the pear.

Local Rule:

Stones in Bunkers
Stones in *bunkers* are movable *obstructions* (Rule 24-1 applies).

I suppose I shouldn't stop recommending which Rules and Decisions to read until you've read all of them, quite obviously each describes something of value that might come up. In fact I *do* recommend that you read them all, but my overriding point is that even if you just carefully read and absorb the few things I've suggested here you will have a very workable background.

Once you begin to see how intricately the Rules are woven together you'll likely be inspired to read more. How they integrate is intriguing. Why are you allowed to remove a discarded bottle cap next to your ball in a bunker, but not allowed to move the half-eaten pear the group in front of you also carelessly tossed right next to it? (Check the Definitions of Obstructions and of Loose Impediments, see in Rule 24-1 that you may always move a Movable Obstruction, and see in Rules 13-4 and 23-1 that you may not move a Loose Impediment in a hazard when your ball is there. Then read Decision 23/3.) Why are you sometimes allowed to move a stone in a bunker that's in the way of your ball, and at other times that little move will cost you two strokes? (Check Rule 13-4c, and Appendix I Part A section "3. Course Conditions" segment "f" and read the optional Local Rule on Stones in Bunkers.) There's consistent logic behind all of this, and it's interesting to see it unfold.

ᛒ

Acknowledging that not everyone will initially care to make a detailed reading of all the Rules, and/or that some people occasionally may be confused when they do, the USGA's website provides a generous number of other learning options. It hosts a dozen videos teaching you how to deal with commonly encountered challenges, quizzes (with answers) which can be sorted into groups of interest to either novices or experienced Rules students, and even a deeply interactive "Rules of Golf Experience" which seamlessly leads you from one place to another. Another option for people particularly attuned to visual learning is a book available on the USGA website, the USGA's *Golf Rules Illustrated.* All in all they offer lots of choices, something for everyone. You can get just a taste or go deep, read or watch and listen, or interact.

While we're talking about the USGA's help in educating people about the Rules, it's also useful to point out that they do an incredible job of reorienting us every time changes are made. For instance, just prior to the latest (2016) version of the Rules of Golf going into effect, the USGA website offered general and specific videos describing the news, "Infographics" picturing relevant revisions, and detailed comparisons of the before/after language used in all the changes.

At the beginning of the latest *Rules of Golf* itself there's a detailed "Principal Changes Introduced in the 2016 Code" section, and a parallel section at the beginning of the *Decisions on the Rules of Golf* book describing "Amendments to 2014 — 2015 Edition" breaking down new Decisions, revised Decisions, re-numbered Decisions and withdrawn Decisions. Pretty darn comprehensive, pretty darn useful, ya gotta love it.

Jumping ahead a couple of holes, an extension of the topic of the USGA preparing us for changes in the Rules is covered extensively in Chapter IV, "A significant Rules proposal for 2019." Almost two full years before the planned adoption of proposed changes, the Ruling Bodies have presented their thinking and asked the public for its reaction.

☙

Back to the current Rules, another interesting way to learn about them is to participate in an online Rules forum. I particularly like the "Rules and Etiquette" section of www.GolfWRX.com. There, on a daily bite-sized basis, you can confer and debate the Rules with amateur golfers, golf pros, and Refs from around the world. The perspective you get by reading the questions and answers, and more importantly tracking the disagreements as they get resolved, can't be beat.

An interesting aspect of reading these online debates is that typically a question is asked by a novice — then another novice may provide an answer that holds a thread of logic but is in fact the wrong answer. Sooner or later someone knowledgeable will step in and cite and explain a specific Rule. The process of first being led down the wrong path and only later getting back on track can do wonders helping you to truly understand the workings of the Rules. And if on rare occasion you still end up confused, the USGA itself can be your resource for clarity.

Most questions have answers already provided on their website, and even if they aren't the USGA welcomes you to submit questions directly to them. You won't enjoy the immediacy of the typically instant response you get from posting on a forum, but at least you'll get the final word right from the start.

⚑

Yet another way to enhance your "hobby" of understanding the Rules of Golf is to read a Rules blog. An excellent one is written by the popular Barry Rhodes, and can be accessed at www.barryrhodes.com. One virtue of Barry's blog is the depth to which he goes in covering a single subject. He'll often look at a topic from several angles, all detailed, and end up providing his readers with a broad perspective that's presented in a way that has a tendency to really stick with you.

⚑

I'd be remiss if I didn't mention that many of the State and Regional Golf Associations affiliated with the USGA host Rules seminars — often for a very modest cost. My Metropolitan Golf Association offered eight in 2016, ranging from an invitation-only Tournament Officials Seminar to Regional Rules Workshops for Rules & Competitions Committee members to several offered to all the members of the MGA — and even one for the general public. In my experience, they're top notch.

⚑

While I wouldn't necessarily recommend it for those who aren't already somewhat comfortable with the Rules, I'd be remiss if I didn't add that the "Ivy League" of Rules education is the three and one half day Rules of Golf Workshop put on jointly by the PGA and the USGA. There are twenty or so Workshops hosted throughout the country each year. They're very comprehensive, very interesting and well worth the time and money.

One of the locations sometimes offered for the Rules of Golf Workshop is the USGA's headquarters in Far Hills, New Jersey. The USGA's golf museum is on that campus as well, and the combination of the workshop and the museum is a nice bonus for anyone who enjoys the history of the game.

The workshop itself consists of three days of lectures from some of the top people in the country, followed by a half day formal exam and a question/answer segment after the exam. The exam itself is very much like the SAT test, both in its multiple-choice structure and in its challenging nature. There are 50 closed-book questions (hopefully answerable from one's basic knowledge gained from the small *Rules of Golf* book) and 50 more difficult open-book questions (for which you may refer to both the small book and your copy of the *Decisions on the Rules of Golf* while taking the remainder of the exam).

Given that many people "self-study" the Rules, it's refreshing to have the most knowledgeable lecturers take you down a path they've marked for you. And having an objective test score to define the level of your progress at the end of the fourth day can be a very useful stake in the ground as you contemplate your new level of expertise. All of which reminds me that the quest for Rules knowledge is more of a journey than a destination. I know a Referee in the UK who is fond of saying, "There are two types of Refs — those that have made mistakes and those that will." I believe it's the ongoing challenge of trying to master that which can't be mastered that keeps us interested in playing golf, and the motivation behind the desire to understand all the nuances in the Rules isn't much different.

♬

At a Workshop I attended at Far Hills, Bernie Loehr, one of my instructors, shared, "We've been answering people's Rules questions for a long, long time. Seldom does a week go by when we don't get a question we've never thought of before." That's the task the USGA and the R&A face every day. Tens of thousands of courses in hundreds of countries around the world, each course significantly different from the next, being played by millions of people requiring consistent, equitable resolutions to myriad problems. It's a staggering undertaking when you think about it, but the R&A and its precursors have resolutely addressed it for almost three hundred years along with the USGA's support for the last 120 or so. All that has led us to the intricate beauty you find in the pages of the *Rules of Golf* today.

III. HOW TO RESOLVE YOUR DIFFERENCES

Trusting that the Rules will treat you well is essential if you expect to build affection for them. But sometimes there's controversy over what is truly fair. In response to that reality, this chapter is a golf lover's equivalent to relationship counseling.

"That's Such A Stupid Rule!"

I wish I had a Pro V1 for every time someone's said that to me. But no harm — when they do, I'm ready: "Do you think so? Tell me why it's stupid."

The fact is, while the specific application of a Rule may sometimes seem odd on the surface, in every case there's a bigger picture to be considered. Don't get me wrong, I'm not saying that the Rules are perfect. (I doubt you could even find someone at the USGA or R&A who would say they are perfect — these same people are on a continual quest to improve them.) I'm simply saying that there is a logical basis for each and every Rule and while some might be improved, the truth is none are "stupid." In fact, discovering the logic that's behind a Rule that you might initially be inclined to view as odd is one of the best ways to end up building respect for the Rules as a whole.

Let me give you an example. In the 1987 Andy Williams Open at Torrey Pines, Craig Stadler's ball ended up underneath a cypress tree. He decided his best shot was to punch out from under a low branch while kneeling, and prior to kneeling down on the wet grass Mr. Stadler famously laid out a towel to protect his pants. He later signed his card, and the next day it came to the attention of officials that he had taken this (illegal) towel action, and he was subsequently disqualified from the tournament for signing an incorrect scorecard. Was that stupid?

Rule:

13-3. Building Stance

A player is entitled to place his feet firmly in taking his *stance*, but he must not build a *stance*.

Decisions:

13-3/2 Making Stroke While Kneeling on Towel

Q. A player's ball was under a tree in such a position that he found it expedient to make his next stroke while on his knees. Because the ground was wet, the player placed a towel on the ground at the spot where his knees would be situated so that the knees of his trousers would not get wet. He then knelt on the towel and made the stroke. Was the player subject to penalty under Rule 13-3 for building a stance?

A. Yes. The same answer would apply if he had wrapped the towel around his knees and knelt on it to make the stroke.

It would have been permissible for the player to have put on waterproof trousers.

1-2/10 Player Wraps Towel Around Self or Places Towel on Cactus Before Taking Stance

Q. A player's ball lies near a cactus, and to play the ball, the player would have to stand with his legs touching the cactus. To protect himself from the cactus needles, the player wraps a towel around his legs before taking his stance. He then plays the ball. What is the ruling?

A. Provided the player does not breach Rule 13-2 (i.e., he takes his stance fairly), there is no breach of the Rules. However, if the player were to place the towel on the cactus, the player would be in breach of Rule 1-2 for altering physical conditions with the intent of affecting the playing of the hole; as a result, he would lose the hole in Match Play or incur a penalty of two strokes in Stroke Play.

It seemed stupid to some people, but let's dig deeper. Rule 13-3 tells us that a player must not "build a stance." The prohibition against building a stance certainly does not in itself seem unreasonable; I doubt anyone would want the game to allow players to drag rocks or logs or kick dirt into a pile to level out their stance or otherwise improve their traction. But in this case Stadler surely wasn't trying to raise the level of his stance or improve the grip of his knees, he was just trying to keep his pants clean. Why hold him responsible for building a stance? The answer is... because writing a Rule which permits some level of stance building and prohibits other levels would create far more confusion and problems than it would solve. Should using one towel underneath your knees be acceptable, but ten or twenty be unacceptable? How about when you're standing in mud? I think it's much more reasonable to always prohibit the act of putting anything down. In that context it's not a stupid Rule, but rather a necessary, practical "line in the sand" that had an unfortunate result for Craig. (A line clearly established by Decision 13-3/2, by the way.) Interestingly, the idea of using clothing or even a towel to protect yourself isn't inherently against the Rules as Decision 1-2/10 clearly shows. But altering the course or building a stance is a different matter!

⚑

The USGA publishes an update of a book originally written decades ago by its former President, Richard S. Tufts, called *THE PRINCIPLES BEHIND The Rules of Golf*. While that book is self-admittedly "on the heavy side," it's equally profound. It introduces us to "The Two Great Principles" of the game: "Play the course as you find it" and "Put your ball in play at the start of the hole, play only your own ball and do not touch it until you lift it from the hole." Adhering to those principles can be challenging — but it is also the basis of what's really fun in the game.

If you page back to the 1744 Leith Links Rules discussed earlier, you'll see that these two principles were evident even back then. It's true that practicality forces us to deviate a bit from the purity of the Principles (for instance the Rules don't make you go swimming around in a Water Hazard to play your ball) but the overriding point here is that the Rules should draw us back to the Principles whenever it is plausible to do so.

Here's a "principle" of mine: Frustration with the Rules of Golf stems "principally" from people's natural desire to stray from the Two Great Principles when they get in a jam. Once the Rules are seen to have made one (very reasonable) concession to circumvent one of the Principles on the basis of practicality, another (perhaps less reasonable) concession is desired. And so it goes until a clearly unreasonable demand is made. The Rules have to draw a line between "reasonable" and "unreasonable" somewhere, and that line is the precise place where friction with the Rules begins. Is some freedom from the Principles appropriate? It sure is. (I don't advocate having to play your ball when it's stuck high up in a tree.) Is total freedom better still? No, of course not, the game would lose its compelling challenge.

Nevertheless to a lot of people the Rules are guilty until proven innocent, so let me give you my take on some of the most common Rules complaints people have. My goal in jumping into the lion's den like this isn't to convince you to "like" the way the Rules are applied in every one of these cases (though that would be nice). More modestly, my goal is to shine a light on the fact that the Rules stand up and face the challenge of drawing a reasonable line in the sand in every one of these matters. I'm hoping after reading this chapter you'll end up agreeing that the Rules do an excellent job of staying balanced and true to themselves in this way. (Actually, they do an excellent job of staying true *to you*, if you'll allow me to expand on my "love the Rules of Golf" metaphor.)

The balance the Rules achieve is particularly impressive when you consider that each specific issue must be considered in context with all the other Rules as the Craig Stadler incident illustrates. Hey, even if you only walk away from this chapter with, "Maybe I wouldn't have written that Rule exactly that way, but at least I see the logic" we'll have accomplished great things.

⚑ ⚑ ⚑

"The Rules Of Golf Are Hopelessly Outdated."

I'm afraid I have to admit that this too-frequently-heard complaint annoys me. The truth is, the Rules we play by today are probably newer than your golf shoes.

The *Rules of Golf* are typically updated every four years, and the *Decisions on the Rules of Golf* every two. On each occasion, all the existing Rules are considered. The USGA's and R&A's committees are constantly reevaluating and debating potential changes, go through an extensive process to make sure any changes are in fact improvements, and do their best to make sure that approved changes don't have unintended consequences.

☙ ☙ ☙

Rule:

6-6. Scoring in Stroke Play
d.   Wrong Score for Hole

The *competitor* is responsible for the correctness of the score recorded for each hole on his score card. If he returns a score for any hole lower than actually taken, he is disqualified. If he returns a score for any hole higher than actually taken, the score as returned stands.

Exception: If a *competitor* returns a score for any hole lower than actually taken due to failure to include one or more *penalty strokes* that, before returning his score card, he did not know he had incurred, he is not disqualified. In such circumstances, the *competitor* incurs the penalty prescribed by the applicable *Rule* and an additional penalty of two strokes for each hole at which the *competitor* has committed a breach of Rule 6-6d. This Exception does not apply when the applicable penalty is disqualification from the competition.

Note 1:   The *Committee* is responsible for the addition of scores and application of the handicap recorded on the score card - see Rule 33-5.

Note 2:   In *four-ball* stroke play, see also Rules 31-3 and 31-7a.

In the most recent iteration of the Rules you'll find reference to the undeniably modern issues of radio-frequency identification chips embedded in golf balls, weather information accessed on multi-functional devices, the use of mobile phones and computers, and listening to music through headphones while playing. (Look up the fairly lengthy Decisions 14-3/14, 14-3/16, 14-3/17 and 14-3/18 and you'll see what I mean.) Without even checking, I'm going to go out on a limb here and say these references were not part of the manuscript when the Ruling Bodies first published unified Rules back in 1952.

As is quite common in Rules updates, fundamental changes to the game have been instituted in the 2016 Rules as well. As one example, a change limiting the possibility of disqualification should a player accidentally return a score lower than actually taken has been adopted as seen in the new Exception listed in Rule 6-6d. (It would have saved Craig Stadler from disqualification!)

Even more topical, on April 25, 2017 the Ruling Bodies instituted mid-year Decision 34-3/10: Limitations on Use of Video Evidence (currently only available for review on their websites), which immediately puts into effect a comforting but somewhat long dissertation confirming that a player's "reasonable judgement" is often sufficient when defining things like where a ball must be replaced or where a ball should be dropped, and expanding upon the existing Decision 18/4 that only video evidence for issues that could be "reasonably seen with the naked eye" should be evaluated in relation to whether a player breached a Rule.

As alluded to earlier, 2017 also marks the year that the Ruling Bodies offer a preview of a Rules Modernization effort they have been jointly working on for adoption in 2019 — further belying the idea that the Rules are a stagnant agency in golf.

I respect a person's right to wish for something different in the Rules. I really do. But I don't respect their right to call the Rules outdated when they're not. (Call them "updated" instead.)

☙ ☙ ☙

Segment of current, 2004 and 2008 Rule:

13-4. Ball in Hazard; Prohibited Actions

Except as provided in the *Rules*, before making a *stroke* at a ball that is in a *hazard* (whether a *bunker* or a *water hazard*) or that, having been lifted from a *hazard*, may be dropped or placed in the *hazard*, the player must not:

a. Test the condition of the *hazard* or any similar *hazard*;

Relevant Exception in 2004 Rule:

None.

Relevant Exception in 2008 Rule:

3. If the player makes a stroke from a hazard and the ball comes to rest in another hazard, Rule 13-4a does not apply to any subsequent actions taken in the hazard from which the stroke was made.

Relevant Exception in current Rule:

2. At any time, the player may smooth sand or soil in a *hazard* provided this is for the sole purpose of caring for the *course* and nothing is done to breach Rule 13-2 with respect to his next *stroke*. If a ball played from a *hazard* is outside the *hazard* after the *stroke*, the player may smooth sand or soil in the *hazard* without restriction.

⚐ ⚐ ⚐

"The Rules Are Way Too Complicated."

While I bristle at the claim that the Rules are outdated, whether they're too complicated or not is a more legitimate debate. They are most certainly complicated, but are they really "too" complicated? In my mind it's more a case of "justifiably complicated" or "necessarily complicated." Maybe I can move you in that direction.

I'm guessing we can all easily agree that having simple Rules is quite a challenge when a sport's playing field is as diverse as it is in golf. Compared to, say, tennis, there's a lot more territory to cover (both literally and figuratively). So the Rules of Golf start off at a bit of a disadvantage compared to the potential for simplicity that other sports enjoy. But that's not the main issue leading me to easily accept the complexity of golf's Rules. Other significant factors are the extraordinarily long period of time during which our Rules have been refined, and the substantial value with which this refinement provides us. Let me give you an example of how that works.

⚐

For ages, the Rules have precluded players from testing the condition of the hazard their ball is in or testing the condition of any similar hazard. (It's kind of a related punishment for being in there in the first place.) Raking the sand in a bunker could certainly provide information as to the condition of the hazard, so that was generally prohibited. Fair enough.

In the 2008 version of the Rules, a gracious Exception was granted (Exception 3) which made a lot of practical sense: If you hit your ball from one bunker into another bunker, you were now allowed to rake the bunker from which you just hit. Faster play, tidier courses, super so far, right?

At the 2008 Zurich Classic, Stewart Cink found his ball just outside a fairway bunker a little less than 200 yards from the green and had to stand in the bunker to make his next shot — which actually ended up in a green-side bunker. Prior to walking to the green, Cink's caddie dutifully raked the fairway bunker.

The next day Cink learned that his caddie's raking of the fairway bunker had been a two-stroke violation of Rule 13-4a, and Mr. Cink was disqualified for having signed a scorecard with a lower score than he was entitled. You see, 2008's Exception 3 only pertained to strokes that went from one hazard to another hazard, and Stewart's ball was not "in" the first hazard — so that Exception did not apply. Ouch!

Pretty much no one thought that outcome was fair, and the Ruling Bodies soon issued a Decision which allowed raking a bunker in this particularly unfortunate circumstance. Then in 2012, when the next new Rule book was published, they revised the Exceptions to Rule 13-4 itself to broaden the allowance even further (see current Exception 2).

This revised Exception 2 requires a bit of thought. You must conclude that the raking was for the sole purpose of caring for the course *and* that nothing was done to violate Rule 13-2 (Improving Lie, Area of Intended Stance or Swing, or Line of Play) to be free from penalty. But on the positive side it's also completely reasonable, workable and fair.

We went from the simplicity of not being allowed to smooth the sand at all if you are in a similar hazard, to being allowed to smooth the sand for a shot going from one hazard to another, to pretty much always being allowed to smooth the sand for the sole purpose of caring for the course. A nice (though perhaps complicated) transition, I think.

The Rule book is filled with invisible tales like this. The next time the complexity of a Rule seems odd to you, consider researching how it came to be. I bet you'll discover that the complexity has value. (No one starts with the goal of making things complicated.)

The bottom line for me? Justice trumps simplicity. (I like justice, and I bet Stewart Cink does too.)

☙ ☙ ☙

Rule:

27-1. Stroke and Distance; Ball Out of Bounds; Ball Not Found Within Five Minutes
a. Proceeding Under Stroke and Distance
At any time, a player may, under penalty of one stroke, play a ball as nearly as possible at the spot from which the original ball was last played (see Rule 20-5), i.e., proceed under penalty of stroke and distance.

Except as otherwise provided in the *Rules*, if a player makes a *stroke* at a ball from the spot at which the original ball was last played, he is deemed to have proceeded under penalty of stroke and distance.

b. Ball Out of Bounds
If a ball is *out of bounds*, the player must play a ball, under penalty of one stroke, as nearly as possible at the spot from which the original ball was last played (see Rule 20-5).

c. Ball Not Found Within Five Minutes
If a ball is *lost* as a result of not being found or identified as his by the player within five minutes after the player's *side* or his or their *caddies* have begun to search for it, the player must play a ball, under penalty of one stroke, as nearly as possible at the spot from which the original ball was last played (see Rule 20-5).

Exception: If it is known or virtually certain that the original ball, that has not been found, has been moved by an *outside agency* (Rule 18-1), is in an *obstruction* (Rule 24-3), is in an *abnormal ground condition* (Rule 25-1) or is in a *water hazard* (Rule 26-1), the player may proceed under the applicable Rule.

Penalty for Breach of Rule 27-1:
Match play - Loss of hole; Stroke play - Two strokes.

Stroke And Distance Penalty

Rule 27-1 covers what we have to do when our ball ends up Out of Bounds. There is absolutely no choice, the Rules tell us we must apply the Stroke and Distance penalty. According to a recent USGA survey the Stroke and Distance penalty is, by a wide margin, the biggest Rules gripe in all of golf. And if this required action for balls which are Out of Bounds isn't traumatic enough on its own, the same Rule applies to lost balls.

People who bristle at this Rule typically cite four objections: it's too punishing, it's too unlike the more flexible penalty for a ball lost in a Water Hazard, it's too time consuming for the player, and it's too annoying to the people behind you when you have to go back to the spot from which you previously played.

⚑

I suspect we can easily agree that Rule 27-1 is punishing; in many cases it's the equivalent of a two stroke penalty. But let's look more closely. Imagine a fairway with Out of Bounds left and a Lateral Water Hazard along the right. If your tee ball ends up Out of Bounds you must take a penalty stroke and re-tee. Let's say your next shot stops in the first cut of rough on the right near the water, where you now lie three. If your first tee shot instead dribbled into the water on the right, and then you chose the two club-length Lateral Water Hazard drop option, you would have ended up lying two in virtually the same place where your re-played Out of Bounds shot ended up in three.

Is it fair that a miscue left would end up costing you one more stroke than a miscue right? It may not only be fair, but actually desirable if you consider the fact that golf is a strategic game, and if you enjoy the related idea that course management is a fundamental part of it. We might not "like" the fact that the OB shot ended up leaving us lying three, but maybe we can appreciate that a different level of danger existing on each side of the fairway makes for a richer, more interesting game.

Almost everyone accepts the penalty for a ball that ends up in a Water Hazard as being appropriate. I think having a different penalty for a ball that ends up Out of Bounds adds to the fun. And even if you don't consider that distinction "fun," shouldn't the penalty for hitting the ball completely off the course be a strong one?

The same thing holds true for losing your ball in the woods or rough. The second of Tufts' "Two Great Principles" referred to earlier tells us that playing a single ball from the tee into the hole is a critical aspect of playing the game. Shouldn't failing to do so come along with a strong penalty — stronger than, for instance, the one-stroke penalty you get for accidentally bumping your ball in the fairway? I think so, and I like to think of the more generous Water Hazard relief options as a bonus rather than thinking of the Lost Ball and Out of Bounds procedure as being overtaxing.

❦ ❦ ❦

Segments of Rules:

27-2. Provisional Ball
a. Procedure

If a ball may be *lost* outside a *water hazard* or may be *out of bounds*, to save time the player may play another ball provisionally in accordance with Rule 27-1. The player must:

i.   announce to his *opponent* in match play or his *marker* or a *fellow-competitor* in stroke play that he intends to play a *provisional ball*; and

ii. play the *provisional ball* before he or his *partner* goes forward to search for the original ball.

If a player fails to meet the above requirements prior to playing another ball, that ball is not a *provisional ball* and becomes the *ball in play* under penalty of stroke and distance (Rule 27-1); the original ball is *lost*.

(Order of play from teeing ground - see Rule 10-3)

Note: If a *provisional ball* played under Rule 27-2a might be *lost* outside a *water hazard* or *out of bounds*, the player may play another *provisional ball*. If another *provisional ball* is played, it bears the same relationship to the previous *provisional ball* as the first *provisional ball* bears to the original ball.

27-1c. Ball Not Found Within Five Minutes

If a ball is *lost* as a result of not being found or identified as his by the player within five minutes after the player's *side* or his or their *caddies* have begun to search for it, the player must play a ball, under penalty of one stroke, as nearly as possible at the spot from which the original ball was last played (see Rule 20-5).

Exception: If it is known or virtually certain that the original ball, that has not been found, has been moved by an *outside agency* (Rule 18-1), is in an *obstruction* (Rule 24-3), is in an *abnormal ground condition* (Rule 25-1) or is in a *water hazard* (Rule 26-1), the player may proceed under the applicable Rule.

Decision:
27-2b/2 When Provisional Ball Holed Becomes Ball in Play

Q.   At a short hole, A's tee shot may be out of bounds or lost, so he plays a provisional ball, which he holes. A does not wish to look for his original ball. B, A's opponent or a fellow-competitor, goes to look for the original ball. When does the provisional ball become the ball in play?

A.   In equity (Rule 1-4) the provisional ball becomes the ball in play as soon as A picks it out of the hole, provided his original ball has not already been found in bounds within five minutes of B starting to search for it.

It might comfort you to know that the Rule-makers have thought long and hard about the implications of Stroke and Distance penalties. They have given serious consideration to the fact that the unpleasant discovery of a ball lying a foot Out of Bounds doesn't just penalize you in terms of your score, but also takes a lot of time to resolve. In a perhaps unappreciated display of compassion, the Ruling Bodies enacted the idea of a Provisional Ball for that very reason. (It's no accident that Rule 27-2 Provisional Ball comes right after Rule 27-1 which covers balls that are Lost or Out of Bounds.)

The sole purpose of the Provisional Ball Rule is to save time — it literally says that in Rule 27-2a. You should note that the establishment of this Rule was a concession. Through its adoption the Ruling Bodies allowed a noteworthy shift away from a fundamental precept in the Rules: they created the unusual circumstance in which you may, on occasion, get to manage whether you'd prefer to continue to play your Provisional Ball (and deliberately not search for your original) or instead search very thoroughly for your original ball (in hopes of being able to avoid having to accept the consequences of a bad Provisional you might have hit).

This departure from the norm can be quite a gift. Say you hit your original into some tall grass, then play a Provisional which clearly goes Out of Bounds. Alternately say you hit your original into that same tall grass, then play a Provisional into the hole! In the first circumstance Rule 27-1c gives you every right to go crazy running around and intensively search for your original ball for a full five minutes to save yourself from having to deal with the consequences of your failed Provisional. In the second circumstance, Decision 27-2b/2 gives you every right to ignore your original ball in the weeds, and instead spend your time sprinting to the hole to pluck the ball out before your Opponent or Fellow Competitor can thwart you by finding your original.

In the midst of my defending the Ruling Bodies' actions regarding the time cost of the Stroke and Distance penalty, let me add that the debate on whether it's too harsh has risen to the very highest levels and has been repeatedly evaluated. In 1960, the USGA established an experimental Rule in which the penalty for a ball Lost or Out of Bounds was reduced to distance only. This experiment was not endorsed by the R&A, and thereby the grand unification of the Rules of the game that was achieved in 1952 was temporarily defeated. That particular experiment was shelved the very next year, but over the following several years other things were tried, including "stroke only" penalties in some situations and the option to enact less-severe Local Rules in others.

After the protracted, multi-continental and painful consideration of all these alternatives, things are now back to where they once were regarding Stroke and Distance. I can't imagine more thorough vetting, and if all that isn't evidence of "fairness" in the Rules, I don't know what is. (If you'd like greater detail about the whys and wherefores of the discontinuance of the USGA's 1960 experimental Rule, Tufts covers it in Appendix II of *The Principles Behind The Rules of Golf*. He calls it, "The Noble Experiment." And If you'd like a more recent treatise on the topic, search "Stroke and Distance Relief" on the USGA's website for a comprehensive 2017 discussion on the matter.)

Despite the preceding discussion, if you're still frustrated by the dictates of the Stroke and Distance penalty there are currently two Rules-abiding workarounds: If you really don't want to go back to the spot from which your original ball was last played, in Match Play you may simply concede the hole to your Opponent (or disqualify yourself from the hole if you are playing with a partner in Best-Ball or Four-Ball) and move on.

If you don't want to go back in individual Stroke Play you'll generally end up disqualified, so the solution is to use the Stableford form of Stroke Play competition described in Rule 32. There, an uncompleted hole simply means you'll earn no points — but you're not disqualified from the competition for failing to finish the hole within the Rules of Golf. Check out the next chapter for a possible third workaround in 2019.

Definition:

Ground Under Repair
"*Ground under repair*" is any part of the *course* so marked by order of the *Committee* or so declared by its authorized representative. All ground and any grass, bush, tree or other growing thing within the *ground under repair* are part of the *ground under repair*. *Ground under repair* includes material piled for removal and a hole made by a greenkeeper, even if not so marked. Grass cuttings and other material left on the *course* that have been abandoned and are not intended to be removed are not *ground under repair* unless so marked.

When the margin of *ground under repair* is defined by stakes, the stakes are inside the *ground under repair*, and the margin of the *ground under repair* is defined by the nearest outside points of the stakes at ground level. When both stakes and lines are used to indicate *ground under repair*, the stakes identify the *ground under repair* and the lines define the margin of the *ground under repair*. When the margin of *ground under repair* is defined by a line on the ground, the line itself is in the *ground under repair*. The margin of *ground under repair* extends vertically downwards but not upwards.

A ball is in *ground under repair* when it lies in or any part of it touches the *ground under repair*.

Stakes used to define the margin of or identify *ground under repair* are *obstructions*.

Note: The Committee may make a Local Rule prohibiting play from ground under repair or an environmentally-sensitive area defined as *ground under repair*.

Decision:
33-8/34 Relief from Divot Holes
Q. May a Committee make a Local Rule providing relief without penalty from divot holes or repaired divot holes (e.g., holes that have been filled with sand and/or seed mix)?
A. No. Such a Local Rule would modify Rule 13-1 and is not authorized.

♟ ♟ ♟

Relief From A Fairway Divot Hole

"I hit an excellent shot to the center of the fairway and it came to rest at the bottom of a divot hole some Bozo failed to fill. I want a free drop. Why do I have to suffer due to someone else's lack of courtesy or the course's lack of maintenance?"

Like the Stroke and Distance controversy, this is an issue with which many people (in this case even one named Jack Nicklaus) find fault. After all, Rule 25-1 gives us free relief from Abnormal Ground Conditions such as Ground Under Repair, so what's up with this? Isn't a fairway divot hole the very definition of Ground Under Repair?

Well... no, it isn't. Unless the Committee explicitly designates the area you're in as Ground Under Repair (or some other Rule happens to intervene) you are obligated to play the ball as it lies. (In fact Decision 33-8/34 says the Committee can't even make a Local Rule to give you universal relief from divot holes.) Rule 13-2 generally prohibits you from improving your lie, and while the Rules do give us free relief from Abnormal Ground Conditions, their goal is to limit that free relief to things that are actually "abnormal." For better or worse, divot holes aren't. In fact you might say they're too common, too "normal."

Nevertheless, the Rules certainly could redefine divot holes as being Ground Under Repair, so why don't they? I'd say the simplest answer to that question resides in the Ruling Bodies' high regard for Great Principle number one, "Play the course as you find it." In fairness, the Rules have already limited adhering to that principle — for instance we are given free relief from Immovable Obstructions like paved cart paths, so why not divot holes too?

One argument lies in the fact that differentiating between artificial constructions like a paved cart path and natural aspects on a course is easy. "Artificial: free relief, Natural: no free relief" is an easy call. But differentiating between two things which are natural, such as a divot hole and a slight depression in the fairway, might not be so easy. Is that depression still a divot hole? Was it ever? How much grass must again be growing before a divot hole turns into just an imperfect lie?

If the Ruling Bodies were to decide to allow you free relief from a divot hole, the definition of an "actionable" divot hole versus any other imperfection would be critical to the fair play of the game. Could such a definition be created? I suppose so. Could it be worded in such a way that all fair-minded players would always make the same Ruling? I doubt it. Sometimes it would be obvious that a ball was in a divot hole, sometimes it wouldn't. (Regrettably, the more frequently players or Refs are forced to make subjective determinations, the more frequently dissatisfaction will occur.)

When you consider the potential time lost in analyzing an imperfect lie in a fairway to determine if it is in fact a divot hole, and then maybe debating it with a Fellow Competitor, Opponent or Ref, and the continuing philosophical goal of playing the course as you find it, the idea of simply requiring you to play from divot holes begins to make sense.

In addition, if the Ruling Bodies were to grant free relief from a lie challenged by the imperfection of a divot hole, some people would next ask for free relief from other imperfections: slight dips, uneven mowing, minor bare spots... the list goes on. Before long we'd be playing a much different game. A less interesting game I think. On the whole I rather like the adventure that random bounces, both favorable and unfavorable, deliver. (In truth, I very much like the favorable bounces, but I don't think it unreasonable for us to be required to take the bad bounces along with them.)

Perhaps I've moved you toward this point of view, but even if I haven't I hope you'll conclude that the decision to leave things as they are is justifiable. And I feel quite certain that if free relief from divot holes is ever granted, Captain of the Golf John Rattray will be shaking his head as he looks down at us from the clouds over Edinburgh, thinking about the uneven lies he used to cheerfully endure.

꩜ ꩜ ꩜

Rule:

Rule 16 - The Putting Green
c. Repair of Hole Plugs, Ball Marks and Other Damage

The player may repair an old *hole* plug or damage to the *putting green* caused by the impact of a ball, whether or not the player's ball lies on the *putting green*. If a ball or ball-marker is accidentally *moved* in the process of the repair, the ball or ball-marker must be replaced. There is no penalty, provided the movement of the ball or ball-marker is directly attributable to the specific act of repairing an old *hole* plug or damage to the *putting green* caused by the impact of a ball. Otherwise, Rule 18 applies.

Any other damage to the *putting green* must not be repaired if it might assist the player in his subsequent play of the hole.

Decisions:

13-2/8 Player's Lie or Line of Play Affected by Pitch-Mark Made by Partner's, Opponent's or Fellow-Competitor's Ball

Q. A player's lie, line of play or area of intended swing through the green is affected by a pitch-mark made by his partner's, his opponent's or a fellow-competitor's ball. Is the player entitled to repair the pitch-mark?

A. If the pitch-mark was there before the player's ball came to rest, he is not entitled to repair it if doing so would improve his lie, line of play, area of intended swing or other area covered by Rule 13-2.

If the pitch-mark was created after the player's ball came to rest, in equity (Rule 1-4), he may repair it. A player is entitled to the lie which his stroke gave him. (Revised)

13-2/8.5 Player's Lie Affected by Sand from Partner's, Opponent's or Fellow-Competitor's Stroke from Bunker

Q. A's ball is on the apron between the green and a bunker. A's partner, opponent or fellow-competitor (B) plays from the bunker and deposits sand on and around A's ball. Is A entitled to any relief?

A. Yes. A is entitled to the lie and line of play he had when his ball came to rest. Accordingly, in equity (Rule 1-4), he is entitled to remove the sand deposited by B's stroke and lift his ball and clean it, without penalty.

⚐ ⚐ ⚐

Repair Of Spike Marks On The Green

"I can fix a ball mark some guy left on the green, but I can't tap down the spike marks the same guy left on my line. Why?" Rule 13-2 prevents us from improving our line of play by "eliminating irregularities of surface." Rule 16-1c provides an exception when it comes to ball marks on the putting green and old hole plugs. So why not spike marks?

This issue is much like the preceding divot hole issue — it's something that the Rules certainly could accommodate, but decide against. The reasoning seems much the same as for divot holes: The Ruling Bodies' desire to lean toward requiring you to play the course as you find it, their desire to speed up play (by disallowing extensive manicuring of long putting lines), and their desire to avoid the expansion of the "I demand that you let me fix it" concept (perhaps to an array of other challenges on the greens like depressions caused by feet or even just inconsistency in grass). Ultimately, I suppose this issue is a perfect example of the "one has to draw the line somewhere" reality, and for better or worse the Ruling Bodies have drawn the line here. (My "friction begins where the line is drawn" principle has no more appropriate example than it does in this particular matter.)

I'll also say that the 2019 Modernization Proposal contemplates allowing relief from spike marks, and if the Ruling Bodies do end up changing this, I'll just as easily live with that allowance as I now easily live with the prohibition. Either way it's reasonable and it's bearable.

As a closing comment I'll add that Decisions 13-2/8 and 13-2/8.5 tell us that we're entitled to the lie and line of play our stroke gave us, so if a player drags his feet across your line <u>after</u> your ball has come to rest, you may in fact legally fix those particular spike marks.

☙ ☙ ☙

Definition:

Nearest Point of Relief

The *"nearest point of relief"* is the reference point for taking relief without penalty from interference by an immovable obstruction (Rule 24-2), *an abnormal ground condition* (Rule 25-1) or a *wrong putting green* (Rule 25-3).

It is the point on the *course* nearest to where the ball lies:

i.   that is not nearer the *hole,* and

ii. where, if the ball were so positioned, no interference by the condition from which relief is sought would exist for the *stroke* the player would have made from the original position if the condition were not there.

Note: In order to determine the nearest point of relief accurately, the player should use the club with which he would have made his next stroke if the condition were not there to simulate the address position, direction of play and swing for such a stroke.

Rules:

24-2. Immovable Obstruction
a. Interference

Interference by an immovable *obstruction* occurs when a ball lies in or on the *obstruction,* or when the *obstruction* interferes with the player's *stance* or the area of his intended swing. If the player's ball lies on the *putting green,* interference also occurs if an immovable *obstruction* on the *putting green* intervenes on his *line of putt.* Otherwise, intervention on the *line of play* is not, of itself, interference under this Rule.

25-1. Abnormal Ground Conditions
a. Interference

Interference by an *abnormal ground condition* occurs when a ball lies in or touches the condition or when the condition interferes with the player's *stance* or the area of his intended swing. If the player's ball lies on the *putting green,* interference also occurs if an *abnormal ground condition* on the *putting green* intervenes on his *line of putt.* Otherwise, intervention on the *line of play* is not, of itself, interference under this Rule.

Note: The *Committee* may make a Local Rule stating that interference by an *abnormal ground condition* with a player's *stance* is deemed not to be, of itself, interference under this Rule.

25-3. Wrong Putting Green
a. Interference
Interference by a *wrong putting green* occurs when a ball is on the *wrong putting green*. Interference to a player's *stance* or the area of his intended swing is not, of itself, interference under this Rule.

Segment of Rule:

20-2. Dropping and Re-Dropping
c. When to Re-Drop
A dropped ball must be re-dropped, without penalty, if it:
v. rolls to and comes to rest in a position where there is interference by the condition from which relief was taken under Rule 24-2b (immovable obstruction), Rule 25-1 (abnormal ground conditions), Rule 25-3 (wrong putting green) or a Local Rule (Rule 33-8a), or rolls back into the pitch-mark from which it was lifted under Rule 25-2 (embedded ball);

Requirement To Take Full Relief

The Definitions tell us that the Nearest Point of Relief is a reference point for taking relief from an Immovable Obstruction, Abnormal Ground Condition, or Wrong Putting Green. It's the nearest point no closer to the hole which eliminates all "interference" from the situation from which relief is being taken (lie, stance and area of intended swing for Immovable Obstructions and Abnormal Ground Conditions, and lie only for Wrong Putting Green). Additionally, Rule 20-2c (v) requires us to re-drop if our dropped ball rolls back into a place where there is once again interference by the condition from which we are taking relief. Consequently, when we choose to take relief from one of these situations, we must end up taking relief from all that is described as interference in Rules 24-2, 25-1 and 25-3. We are required to take "full relief."

All of that seems fine and dandy until we note that sometimes people take a drop motivated by an unattractive lie or line of play, but when they do they fail to simultaneously take relief for part of their stance as well. There was a noteworthy incident in this regard at the 2014 European Tour event in Abu Dhabi, in which Rory McIlroy chose to take relief from a spectator pathway marked with a white line as Ground Under Repair. He took his drop, and checked to see that his ball came to rest outside the marked area, but when he subsequently took his stance and struck his ball his foot was still within the area marked Ground Under Repair. He was later penalized, and criticized the Rule in part because he did not get any advantage by having his foot remain in the Ground Under Repair.

So, is this Rule in fact unfair? To judge that, let's take a look at it from this point of view: The Rules provided the player with the option to play the ball as it lied, and they provided him with another option to take a free drop outside the marked area. But when the Rules provide you with a free drop, they don't allow you to drop anywhere you choose — they carefully prescribe where that drop may be taken. It's the player's job to decide whether he wants to play from his current position or to play from another legal area. I'd hope we can all easily agree that once the player drops he shouldn't get a choice as to whether that new place is appealing — he should simply make sure the drop was legal and then have to deal with it.

In this case, Rory's drop ended up in an area that was inappropriate due to his stance. His only choice was to re-drop. Did he get an advantage from playing from the illegal position? Almost certainly not, but we'll never really know, because we don't know where the next drop would have ended up. Maybe it would have landed in a depression or against a rock. So even though he said he didn't get an advantage in playing from the wrong place, and even though I'm sure he was sincere in that belief, he can't really know that to be true.

Taking this away from the specific incident, what the Rules say is "fair" is that if you want to take a free drop, you don't subsequently get to decide if you want to do it over again based on whether you like your new position or your new lie. You don't get another bite at the apple — if your ball is in a legal place you must deal with it, if it isn't you must address that. A player who insists that he should be permitted to violate that principle based on whether or not he believes there's "an advantage" is a player who believes he should be allowed to subjectively decide the point from which his ball will next be played. The Rules disagree with that, they tell you where you may drop, and via Rule 20-2c they also provide a list of circumstances in which you must drop again.

The requirement to take full relief might sometimes help a player, might sometimes hurt him, but always takes the player's whim out of the equation. I'm good with that.

☙ ☙ ☙

Definition:

Rub of the Green
A *"rub of the green"* occurs when a ball in motion is accidentally deflected or stopped by any *outside agency* (see Rule 19-1).

Rules:

Rule 23 - Loose Impediments
23-1. Relief
Except when both the *loose impediment* and the ball lie in or touch the same *hazard,* any *loose impediment* may be removed without penalty.

If the ball lies anywhere other than on the *putting green* and the removal of a *loose impediment* by the player causes the ball to *move,* Rule 18-2 applies.

On the *putting green,* if the ball or ball-marker is accidentally *moved* in the process of the player removing a *loose impediment,* the ball or ball-marker must be replaced. There is no penalty, provided the movement of the ball or ball-marker is directly attributable to the removal of the *loose impediment.* Otherwise, the player incurs a penalty of one stroke under Rule 18-2.

When a ball is in motion, a *loose impediment* that might influence the movement of the ball must not be removed.

Note: If the ball lies in a *hazard,* the player must not touch or move any *loose impediment* lying in or touching the same *hazard* - see Rule 13-4c.

Penalty for Breach of Rule:
Match play - Loss of hole; Stroke play - Two strokes.

Rule 28 - Ball Unplayable

The player may deem his ball unplayable at any place on the *course*, except when the ball is in a *water hazard*. The player is the sole judge as to whether his ball is unplayable.

If the player deems his ball to be unplayable, he must, under penalty of one stroke:

a. Proceed under the stroke and distance provision of Rule 27-1 by playing a ball as nearly as possible at the spot from which the original ball was last played (see Rule 20-5); or
b. Drop a ball behind the point where the ball lay, keeping that point directly between the hole and the spot on which the ball is dropped, with no limit to how far behind that point the ball may be dropped; or
c. Drop a ball within two club-lengths of the spot where the ball lay, but not nearer the hole.

If the unplayable ball is in a *bunker*, the player may proceed under Clause a, b or c. If he elects to proceed under Clause b or c, a ball must be dropped in the *bunker*.

When proceeding under this Rule, the player may lift and clean his ball or *substitute* a ball.

Penalty for Breach of Rule:
Match play - Loss of hole; Stroke play - Two strokes.

Decision:
23/2 Meaning of "Solidly Embedded" in Definition of "Loose Impediments"

Q. The Definition of "Loose Impediments" states that a stone is a loose impediment if it is not "solidly embedded." When is a stone solidly embedded?

A. If a stone is partially embedded and may be picked up with ease, it is a loose impediment. When there is doubt as to whether a stone is solidly embedded or not, it should not be removed.

⚑ ⚑ ⚑

Tree Roots, Stones, Hardpan And Rubs Of The Green

The last topic I'll cover regarding the general concept of fairness in the Rules can be lumped into the category of "bad breaks." (A Rub of the Green is technically when your moving golf ball is interfered with by an Outside Agency such as a bird, but as we all know any sort of unanticipated bounce can lead to frustration.) I'm not bringing up bad breaks so much because the topic really needs Rules insight to clarify it, but simply because bad breaks generate so much irritation.

We all readily accept the bounce off a tree that ends up leaving our ball back in the fairway. And most of us (begrudgingly) accept responsibility for the bounce off a tree that leaves us deeper in the woods. But for some reason or other, there are a lot of people who bristle when finding their ball lying on stones, hardpan or trapped between tree roots in the rough. Somehow these shots, even though errant, are seen as deserving special dispensation. Amidst the cussing and fuming, you'll hear expressions of anger directed at the course superintendent, claims of victimization by the golf gods, pretext regarding fear of injury, and finally the ritual damning of the Rules of Golf. At that moment these souls feel the phrase "play the course as you find it" is not an intriguing challenge but rather an unbearable burden.

To these people I say, "I'm truly sorry for your misfortune. I've often been there myself. And I sincerely don't want you to hurt yourself. Nor do the Rules of Golf, which have responsibly provided relief possibilities for you under the several options within the Unplayable Ball Rule 28 at the cost of just a single stroke." Come on folks, the Loose Impediment Rule 23 provides you with the possibility of free relief via carefully removing stones or other Loose Impediments. And you can even remove partially-embedded impediments as long as they can be picked up "with ease" and you don't accidentally move your ball. (Decision 23/2 confirms that.) If you're in such a mess that these free options don't help, isn't it fair to think of the problem as one for which you should take responsibility?

I'll conclude my dissertation on bad breaks and the concept of fairness with an observation that's equally valid for all problem circumstances encountered on the golf course: As long as we all know and play by the same Rules, the Rules of Golf are inherently fair because they treat us all the same. You might have to deal with a random bounce that leaves you nestled deep in a gnarly tree root with no free relief, and so might I. Concluding that the Rules have therefore treated us both fairly isn't really any more complicated than that. And with that bit of obvious profundity, we'll move on to review how the Rules are in the process of introspectively questioning themselves, and might change significantly in 2019.

⚑ ⚑ ⚑

IV. A SIGNIFICANT RULES PROPOSAL FOR 2019

As the preceding chapter chronicled, some people have consternation about some of the Rules. Beyond that, as we've also discussed, Rules often lead to the need for clarifying Decisions and over time things build up, get multi-layered and complicated.

Every now and then a responsible party might ask, "While things are indeed refined, shouldn't we step back, take a look at where we are, and see if there is an easier-to-implement, less complicated, more consistent, fresh way to look at things?"

Well, on March 1, 2017, that's exactly what the Ruling Bodies proposed: A Rules Modernization Initiative which they began developing in 2012 that reviewed all aspects of the Rules without bias as to what currently exists, and which describes a startlingly broad array of possible changes.

While such substantial rethinking by the Ruling Bodies is infrequent, previous efforts resulted in comprehensive Rules changes published in 1899 (soon after the founding of the USGA), 1934 (a major effort to clarify the Rules), 1952 (the establishment of a unified code reconciling differences between the R&A's and USGA's perspective on the base Rules), and in 1984 (when the Decisions on the Rules of Golf were finally unified as well).

This time the Ruling Bodies have proposed profound changes ranging from the structure, number and titles of the various Rule books to the style of language, illustrations and photographs within them, to surprising procedural changes we might be using to execute fundamental tasks. It's an amazingly formidable effort, particularly when you note that despite all of the proposed changes, the principles of our game solidly remain.

The timing for this task seems well thought out:

March 1, 2017: detailed presentation of the proposal and request for public feedback
August 31, 2017: feedback period ends
Winter 2018: review feedback, approve new Rules
Spring 2018: announce final determinations/begin education efforts
January 1, 2019: new Rules go into effect

⚐

So, what's the real deal here? Beyond the structure and style of the proposed new Rule books there are more than 30 "major changes" being put forward. To me, some particularly enticing ones include:

- Dropping from any height you wish, even less than an inch above the ground, but requiring that the ball end up staying within the sanctioned drop area (instead of having to follow the complexity of current Rule 20-2c to figure out if a re-drop is required if it bounces out).
- Dropping within an arc 20 inches to the side or behind a spot from which a ball was last played instead of having to drop "as close as possible" to that specific spot (which too often requires a re-drop when a ball bounces modestly closer to the hole than that small spot).
- Allowing Committees to define any area of the course, whether it meets the current Definition of a Water Hazard or not, as a "Penalty Zone" (functionally permitting the legal use of most of today's Water Hazard relief options in areas other than Water Hazards and potentially speeding up play).
- Authorizing an optional Stroke Play format where you may pick up your ball and record a "Maximum Score" instead of having to hole out (thereby providing the option of avoiding walking back for a Stroke and Distance penalty).
- Removing the penalty if you accidentally move your ball during a search, or if your ball accidentally hits you or your equipment while in motion after a stroke.
- Permitting your putt to hit an unattended flagstick in the hole.

Naturally, the proposed changes go far beyond my "most enticing" list here, and I heartily encourage you to visit the USGA's (or R&A's) website to review all the in-depth resources they've provided associated with the proposal. The proposed Rules themselves are there along with explanatory videos, comparison charts, and white papers describing the Ruling Bodies' thinking on several matters. There's even discussion on why certain topics are not currently being proposed for change (Stroke and Distance penalty and free relief from divot holes in fairways for example) though even those topics may be revisited before this exercise is complete.

⚑

On a personal note, there's nothing more appealing to me than the powers that be making modifications to the Rules which naturally lead players to avoid unintended violations — as long as those modifications don't degrade the principles of the game, don't fundamentally make golf easier, and don't fundamentally drive scores lower. (I adore the challenge of golf, I've got a lifetime of "data" identifying what is and what is not a good round for me, a lifetime of data identifying just how impressed I should be by a pro's score, and for the life of me I don't want to have to vacate all of my associated emotions.) But outside a few quibbles I have here or there, I'm intrigued by this comprehensive proposal and what it might mean for us all.

Perhaps the best part of the Ruling Bodies' plan is their openness to gathering feedback from all of us. On the USGA website you'll find directions as to how you can have your voice heard. In particular, you'll find a Feedback Survey that is both interesting and easy to navigate. It permits you to offer your subjective opinion on dozens of questions, and allows you to supplement your response with comments if you wish.

The Rules are reaching out to you, it's a wonderful time to fall in love with them.

V. HOW TO USE THE RULES FOR YOUR OWN SELFISH PURPOSES

Some Secrets To Scoring Your Best

Here's the most seductive way of all to end up loving the Rules of Golf: Let them serve you.

I may be accused of being the Apostle of the Obvious here, but I'll start off by saying that knowing the Rules inherently gives you an edge — you get protected from committing needless violations. But less obvious is the fact that knowing the Rules delivers many affirmative advantages.

There are vast numbers of ways in which sometimes fairly straightforward, sometimes quirky explorations into the Rules can help you. Let's delve into both, and exploit the "secrets" this study reveals.

Interact With A Referee

Even if you're an absolute ace with the Rules, when you find yourself in a competition and there's a Referee at hand who asks if you'd like to hear your options, I strongly suggest you say, "Yes, please tell me." It doesn't cost you anything to hear him or her out, and more importantly there's a reasonable chance that the Ref may be aware of something that you aren't.

We Refs live in a bit of an odd space. We walk around the course concentrating on the Rules of Golf, unencumbered by competing concerns players must deal with like course management and making a good stroke. Refs are inherently paying attention to details for which you probably don't have as much time. And we might have spent much of the day studying the one particular hole you're now playing.

We try to get ourselves in a position where we can easily see players in order to help them, but we also try not to get so close that we might distract them or add tension. We don't want to interrupt your rhythm, but we will be disappointed if you end up incurring a penalty that we could have helped you avoid. We can't make playing suggestions, but we do want to be of assistance to the extent we are permitted. If one of us actually speaks to you while you're playing, there's a solid chance that we have something valuable for you to consider. "Would you like to hear your options?" could very well be code for "What the hell are you about to do?" or "Oh my, it seems like you're about to make a really peculiar choice!"

❧ ❧ ❧

Definition:

Loose Impediments

"*Loose impediments*" are natural objects, including:

- stones, leaves, twigs, branches and the like,
- dung, and
- worms, insects and the like, and the casts and heaps made by them, provided they are not:
  - fixed or growing,
  - solidly embedded, or
  - adhering to the ball.

Sand and loose soil are *loose impediments* on the *putting green*, but not elsewhere.

Snow and natural ice, other than frost, are either *casual water* or *loose impediments*, at the option of the player.

Dew and frost are not *loose impediments*.

Decisions:

23-1/2 Large Stone Removable Only with Much Effort

Q. A player's ball lies in the rough directly behind a loose stone the size of a watermelon. The stone can be removed only with much effort. Is it a loose impediment which may be removed?

A. Yes. Stones of any size (not solidly embedded) are loose impediments and may be removed, provided removal does not unduly delay play (Rule 6-7).

23-1/3 Assistance in Removing Large Loose Impediment

Q. May spectators, caddies, fellow-competitors, etc. assist a player in removing a large loose impediment?

A. Yes.

34-2/2 Referee Authorizes Player to Infringe a Rule

Q. In error, a referee authorized a player to infringe a Rule of Golf. Is the player absolved from penalty in such a case?

A. Yes. Under Rule 34-2, a referee's decision is final, whether or not the decision is correct.

I was officiating at a tournament recently in which a skilled amateur friend of mine was competing. I was stationed at the 18th hole. My friend pulled his drive, and I went over to help search for his ball which I found near a group of large stones. The rocks were sitting in un-mowed grass, so you couldn't easily see that they weren't actually embedded in the ground. One of the (18 inch or so diameter) stones impeded my friend's backswing, and he was carefully taking slow motion practice swings to feel out how steep a downswing he'd have to manufacture in order to miss the stone and still make solid contact with his ball. All the while I was thinking to myself, "Dude! Even though that stone is pretty big, I checked before you got here and saw it's not solidly embedded. It's a Loose Impediment and you're allowed to remove it!"

Unfortunately, while warning a player about a potential Rules violation is clearly part of my job, suggesting playing strategies is absolutely not — that's the caddie's or partner's role in life. There was no potential Rules violation looming in front of my friend so all I could legitimately do was stand there and watch. (Though I'll admit I was sending any number of failed telepathic messages hoping he would take a step back and take a fresh look at what he was doing.)

I really do wish he asked me to describe his options regarding that stone. His shot didn't work out that well for him.

All of which reminds me of Tiger getting that crowd in Phoenix to roll that huge boulder out of the way for him. (So as not to rekindle controversy, Decisions 23-1/2 and 23-1/3 explicitly allowed Tiger to move that stone with the help of his supporters. It surprises some people that the right to move the stone was already on the books prior to the incident, but it was. And further, Tiger cleared the process with a Ref before he engaged in it. I file the episode under "smart golf.")

♜

You've undoubtedly noted that many Touring Pros involve themselves with Refs over seemingly obvious issues. Part of that is concern about expensive mistakes the player might make regarding a Rule, and part could be a desire to have other options brought to the player's attention as I just mentioned, but there's another important aspect of this type of exchange: If a Ref offers you an option that's attractive, and you use it but it's later discovered to have been illegal, you've got no worries. Having had that action cleared in advance by the Ref gives you a very nice get-out-of-jail-free card according to Decision 34-2/2.

❦ ❦ ❦

Rule:

25-2. Embedded Ball

If a player's ball is embedded in any closely-mown area *through the green*, it may be lifted, cleaned and dropped, without penalty, as near as possible to the spot where it lay but not nearer the *hole*. The ball when dropped must first strike a part of the *course through the green*.

Note 1:   A ball is "embedded" when it is in its own pitch-mark and part of the ball is below the level of the ground. A ball does not necessarily have to touch the soil to be embedded (e.g., grass, *loose impediments* and the like may intervene between the ball and the soil).

Note 2:   "Closely-mown area" means any area of the *course*, including paths through the rough, cut to fairway height or less.

Note 3:   The *Committee* may adopt the Local Rule as provided for in Appendix I allowing a player relief, without penalty, for a ball embedded anywhere *through the green*.

Local Rule:

Embedded Ball

Through the green, a ball that is embedded may be lifted, cleaned and dropped, without penalty, as near as possible to the spot where it lay but not nearer the *hole*. The ball when dropped must first strike a part of the *course through the green*.

Note: A ball is "embedded" when it is in its own pitch-mark and part of the ball is below the level of the ground. A ball does not necessarily have to touch the soil to be embedded (e.g., grass, *loose impediments* and the like may intervene between the ball and the soil).

Exceptions:
1. A player may not take relief under this Local Rule if the ball is embedded in sand in an area that is not closely-mown.
2. A player may not take relief under this Local Rule if interference by anything other than the condition covered by this Local Rule makes the *stroke* clearly impracticable.

Penalty For Breach Of Local Rule:

Match play - Loss of hole; Stroke play - Two strokes.

Check For Local Rules

There is great variance in the level of attention Course Committees and Competition Committees pay to invoking and communicating Local Rules, and to pointing out noteworthy idiosyncrasies of a course. If a tournament in which you are playing offers a Local Rules sheet, it could be critical that you read it, irrespective of how much you already know about the Rules in general. (Just ask Dustin Johnson if he wishes he had thoroughly studied the material provided to him about the bunkers at Whistling Straits before the 2010 PGA Championship. His grounding his club in that bunker he didn't think was a bunker on 18 not only hurt him, but everyone who was watching.)

Even if you're not playing a tournament, but simply embrace the idea of playing by the Rules, checking for Local Rules can be rewarding. It used to be harder to get apprised of which Local Rules are in effect at an unfamiliar course, but things are improving. Asking the pro or the starter has always been a possibility, but that can be a hit-or-miss proposition. You'll sometimes find Local Rules on the scorecard (at least permanent ones, though of course not ones based on the day's conditions). The biggest improvement is that now it's more and more likely that you can find detailed Local Rules listed online on the course's website. Sometimes Local Rules provide you with privileges you wouldn't otherwise enjoy, so by all means check them out.

When you do so, don't be surprised if you fail to find something you'd expect to be there. For instance, while the legal use of Distance Measuring Devices is certainly widespread, that doesn't mean a Committee has taken the necessary step of providing for their use via adopting the Local Rule, so check to be sure.

The U.S.'s PGA Tour events all adopt the "Embedded Ball" Local Rule. So some people, particularly those of us who watch pro golf on TV in the United States, may not realize that the Embedded Ball Rule 25-2 does not permit free relief from a plugged ball in the rough — it only applies to closely mown areas of the course (that are not in hazards). The Embedded Ball Local Rule expands the relief to all areas Through the Green (as long as you're not embedded in sand in an area that's not closely-mown). Unless you're really good at hitting an Embedded Ball or enjoy Unplayable Ball penalties, you'll want to know if this Local Rule is in force.

❦ ❦ ❦

Local Rules:

Stones in Bunkers
Stones in *bunkers* are movable *obstructions* (Rule 24-1 applies)

Accidental Movement of a Ball on a Putting Green
Rules 18-2, 18-3 and 20-1 are modified as follows:

When a player's ball lies on the putting green, there is no penalty if the ball or ball-marker is accidentally moved by the player, his partner, his opponent, or any of their caddies or equipment.

The moved ball or ball-marker must be replaced as provided in Rules 18-2, 18-3 and 20-1.

This Local Rule applies only when the player's ball or ball-marker lies on the putting green and any movement is accidental.

Note: If it is determined that a player's ball on the putting green was moved as a result of wind, water or some other natural cause such as the effects of gravity, the ball must be played as it lies from its new location. A ball-marker moved in such circumstances is replaced.

Another helpful Local Rule you might discover is the Stones in Bunkers Local Rule, in which you can treat a stone in a bunker as a Movable Obstruction — allowing free relief from what is ordinarily a Loose Impediment even though you're in a hazard. You can even accidentally bump your ball penalty-free when removing the stone (as you can in removing any Movable Obstruction).

℔

Perhaps the Big Kahuna of Local Rules to look for is the new 2017 option: "Accidental movement of a ball on a putting green." It provides free relief for the unsettling experience of a player accidentally causing his ball to move while doing things like addressing his ball, making a practice swing, and dropping his ball on his marker or his marker on his ball when he's on the green.

℔

There are lots of other advantages you might discover when you check out the Local Rules for a course. The presence of Water Hazard Dropping Zones (good to know about before you drop via another relief option — it's pretty frustrating when you didn't know a Zone was there and then you walk past it as you approach the green after it's too late), the opportunity to get free relief from a flower bed or a young tree, the right to hit a Provisional Ball even if you think your original may be in a Water Hazard — the possibilities go on and on... if you bother to check you might even get treated to preferred lies.

Definition:

Committee

The "*Committee*" is the committee in charge of the competition or, if the matter does not arise in a competition, the committee in charge of the *course*.

Segment of Rule:

Rule 33 - The Committee
33-2. The Course
a. Defining Bounds and Margins

The *Committee* must define accurately:
  i.   the course and out of bounds,
  ii. the margins of water hazards and lateral water hazards,
  iii. ground under repair , and
  iv. *obstructions* and integral parts of the *course*.

33-8. Local Rules
a. Policy

The *Committee* may establish Local Rules for local abnormal conditions if they are consistent with the policy set forth in Appendix I.

b. Waiving or Modifying a Rule

A Rule of Golf must not be waived by a Local Rule. However, if a *Committee* considers that local abnormal conditions interfere with the proper playing of the game to the extent that it is necessary to make a Local Rule that modifies the Rules of Golf, the Local Rule must be authorized by the USGA.

Decision:

33-2a/2 Declaring Area as Ground Under Repair During Competition Round

Q. A's ball is in a poor lie in a washed-out area which warrants being marked as ground under repair but is not so marked. He deems the ball unplayable and proceeds under Rule 28, incurring a one-stroke penalty. Subsequently, in the same competition round, B's ball is in the same area. B requests the Committee to declare the area ground under repair. Would the Committee be justified in declaring the area ground under repair in such circumstances?

A. Yes; this applies in either match or stroke play. However, it is preferable that all areas which warrant marking as ground under repair should be so marked before the start of a competition.

☗ ☗ ☗

Take Charge

The Definitions tell us that the Committee is the entity in charge of a competition. If there's no formal competition being held, the Committee in charge of the golf course determines the specifics of how your game must be played.

Rule 33 describes some of the Committee's responsibilities which importantly include deciding which Local Rules should be adopted and what areas should be considered Ground Under Repair. Rule 34 goes on to empower the Committee to resolve disputes. All important stuff!

During casual play things can be frustrating for players who don't have ready access to a Committee or a Ref: Is today's rain sufficient to have our round played under the Preferred Lies Local Rule? Should that bare spot in the fairway be considered Ground Under Repair? Is Sam's ball actually on the putting green? These aren't trivial issues, and if you're devoted to playing by the Rules they have to be resolved. Particularly in the case of determining which Local Rules should be adopted for the day, seeking the Committee's advice after the round just doesn't work. So almost everyone just slogs on. But what else might the devoted Rules fan do?

Well, if it's impractical or impossible to contact the Course Committee, you can form a Competition Committee yourself. In fact, the technical requirements are modest. To be a legitimate Competition Committee you must simply be presiding over a competition of two or more people and set up your Committee prior to the start of play. Before you tee off determine what form of play your group is planning, decide which Local Rules you want to enact and how you'll deal with ties, and have at it! While you should not change any Local Rules during the competition, Decision 33-2a/2 gives you authority to make calls regarding Ground Under Repair while on the fly.

As long as you clear up in advance who is on the Committee and what roles they'll play in making rulings, you should be good to go.

As a word of caution, the duties of a Competition Committee are extensive. It's likely that nothing confounding will interfere with you and your friends having a fine day, but it's not guaranteed. Study the Rules and Decisions surrounding Rule 33 and 34 to get a better idea of the obligations of the Committee and the limits to its authority before you take the plunge!

(If you really want to get serious about this, get yourself a copy of the USGA's booklet, *How to Conduct a Competition*.)

☙ ☙ ☙

Rule:

26-1. Relief for Ball in Water Hazard

It is a question of fact whether a ball that has not been found after having been struck toward a *water hazard* is in the *hazard*. In the absence of knowledge or virtual certainty that a ball struck toward a *water hazard*, but not found, is in the *hazard*, the player must proceed under Rule 27-1.

If a ball is found in a *water hazard* or if it is known or virtually certain that a ball that has not been found is in the *water hazard* (whether the ball lies in water or not), the player may under penalty of one stroke:

a.   Proceed under the stroke and distance provision of Rule 27-1 by playing a ball as nearly as possible at the spot from which the original ball was last played (see Rule 20-5); or

b.   Drop a ball behind the *water hazard*, keeping the point at which the original ball last crossed the margin of the *water hazard* directly between the *hole* and the spot on which the ball is dropped, with no limit to how far behind the *water hazard* the ball may be dropped; or

c.   As additional options available only if the ball last crossed the margin of a *lateral water hazard*, drop a ball outside the *water hazard* within two club-lengths of and not nearer the *hole* than (i) the point where the original ball last crossed the margin of the *water hazard* or (ii) a point on the opposite margin of the *water hazard* equidistant from the *hole*.

When proceeding under this Rule, the player may lift and clean his ball or *substitute* a ball.

(Prohibited actions when ball is in a hazard - see Rule 13-4)
(Ball moving in water in a water hazard - see Rule 14-6)

Decisions:

26-1/14 Clarification of "Opposite Margin" in Rule 26-1c(ii)

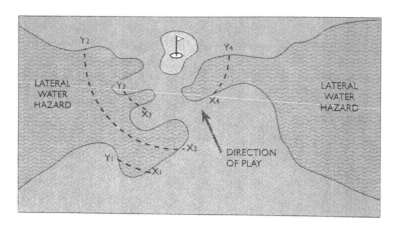

Q. Please clarify the words "opposite margin" in Rule 26-1c. With regard to the diagram, "X1" indicates where a ball in the hazard last crossed the hazard margin. May the player drop a ball within two club-lengths of "Y1"? And, may a player whose ball last crossed the hazard margin at "X2" drop a ball within two club-lengths of "Y2," and so on?

A. With respect to "X1," "Y1" is "a point on the opposite margin of the water hazard equidistant from the hole." Accordingly, the player would be entitled to drop a ball within two club-lengths of "Y1."

The same applies in the cases of "X3"-"Y3" and "X4"-"Y4," but not in the case of "X2"-"Y2." A "point on the opposite margin" is a point across the hazard from "the point where the original ball last crossed the margin of the hazard." "Y2" is not across the hazard from "X2" because an imaginary straight line from "X2" to "Y2" crosses land outside the hazard.

26-1/15 Procedures for Relief from Lateral Water Hazard

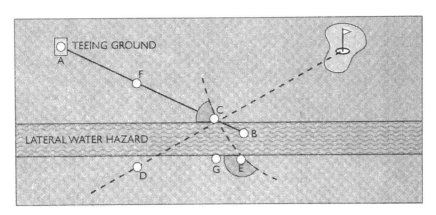

In the diagram, a player has played a ball from the teeing ground (Point A) into the lateral water hazard at Point B. It last crossed the margin of the hazard at Point C. He may play the ball as it lies or, under penalty of one stroke:

a. play another ball from the teeing ground - Rule 26-1a;

b. drop a ball anywhere on the far side of the hazard on the dotted line from the hole through Point C, e.g., Point D - Rule 26-1b;

c. drop a ball in the shaded area on the near side of the hazard which is all ground within two club-lengths of Point C, but not nearer the hole than Point C - Rule 26-1c(i); or

d. drop a ball in the shaded area on the far side of the hazard which is all ground within two club-lengths of Point E, but not nearer the hole than Point E - Rule 26-1c(ii).

The player may not drop a ball on the so-called "line-of-flight" at Point F or anywhere else on the line the ball followed from A to B, except in the shaded area on the near side. Nor may he drop a ball within two club-lengths of Point G, the point on the far side of the hazard directly opposite Point C.

Navigate Water Hazards

Losing your ball in a Water Hazard is one of the most common causes of having to take a drop. Rule 26-1a and 26-1b detail the two relief options for Water Hazards and Rule 26-1c adds two additional Lateral Water Hazard options to the wise player's repertoire. Yet the last of these options, 26-1c (ii), is largely ignored by amateur players. This Rule allows you to drop within two club-lengths of and not nearer the hole than "a point on the opposite margin of the water hazard equidistant from the hole." Why should you bother to figure out what that means? Because on occasion it can provide you with an extraordinary advantage.

Before availing yourself of such a right, get clear on precisely what "opposite margin" means: Take a moment and study the words and drawing provided in Decision 26-1/14. It may take a little while to follow the various scenarios, but when you do you'll see that, for instance, choosing to drop near point Y4 instead of X4 allows you to legally pitch your next shot to the green without having to risk going over the water again. If the only relief option you consider is dropping within two club-lengths of the last point your ball crossed the margin of the hazard (X4), you may be giving up that "no-more-water-in-my-way" option. That can be a reckless decision — take it from someone who has put two consecutive balls in a Lateral Water Hazard from within 50 yards of the flagstick once or twice.

And it's not only freedom from having to hit a second shot over water that's at stake. With Lateral Water Hazards it's not uncommon to have one of the hazard's margins populated by trees with potentially interfering branches, and it's also not uncommon to end up with a downhill lie after your drop near one margin when you'd instead end up with an uphill lie if you drop near the other. Take a moment and consider all of that next time you're in a Match. You might not only get yourself a better result, but you might throw your befuddled Opponent into a tailspin as well. Not a bad dividend for studying a little drawing. If I've sold you on that, while you're in study mode carefully read the next Decision as well, 26-1/15. It will help drive the whole lesson home.

♫ ♫ ♫

While I'm musing about Water Hazard drops, let me offer another observation and related suggestion for your consideration. We've already discussed the fact that when you take a drop from an Abnormal Ground Condition or Immovable Obstruction, you must end up finding the nearest point of complete relief, including relief for your stance. Go back and read Rule 26-1 and you'll see that unlike Abnormal Ground Condition Rule 25-1a and Obstruction Rule 24-2a in which the description of interference includes your stance, the Water Hazard Rule does not mention your stance and does not refer in any way to the Nearest Point of Relief. It's only the ball's position inside or outside the margin of the hazard and the point it last crossed the hazard margin that is at issue, and consequently the Ruling Bodies don't care a whit about where your feet are when you later take your stance.

That "freedom" regarding your stance can end up hurting you. It's pretty common to have the ground around a Water Hazard or Lateral Water Hazard slope steeply toward the hazard line, so if possible you should take care that your dropped ball doesn't bounce toward the hazard in such a way that you'll have to stand on the sloppy ground (or even in the water) within the hazard when you take your next shot. Don't forget, while Rule 20-2c (i) allows you (actually, requires you) to drop again if your ball "rolls into and comes to rest in a hazard," it doesn't provide a second chance just because your ball rolls up close to the edge of the hazard line where your feet might end up wet — or where a bush within the hazard might interfere with your swing. So, being aware of these unpleasant potentialities, what can you do? Answer: be careful where, and in what manner, you drop.

꘎ ꘎ ꘎

Rule:

20-2. Dropping and Re-Dropping
a. By Whom and How

A ball to be dropped under the *Rules* must be dropped by the player himself. He must stand erect, hold the ball at shoulder height and arm's length and drop it. If a ball is dropped by any other person or in any other manner and the error is not corrected as provided in Rule 20-6, the player incurs a penalty of one stroke.

If the ball, when dropped, touches any person or the *equipment* of any player before or after it strikes a part of the course and before it comes to rest, the ball must be re-dropped, without penalty. There is no limit to the number of times a ball must be re-dropped in these circumstances.

(Taking action to influence position or movement of ball - see Rule 1-2)

Decision:

20-2a/2 Spinning Ball When Dropping

Q. A player puts spin on a ball purposely when dropping it. What is the ruling?

A. The player incurs a penalty of one stroke under Rule 20-2a for dropping the ball in an improper manner, unless he corrects his mistake as permitted by Rule 20-6.

Where to drop is obvious given the dangers we've been discussing (as far from a challenging hazard line as is legal/useful), but what may be less obvious is that you have some choice over the manner in which you drop. More precisely, you frequently have a bit of control over how far a ball might bounce after it hits the course. Here's what I mean: Rule 20-2a tells us how to drop. We must stand erect and extend our dropping hand at shoulder height and arm's length before we let go of the ball. While Decision 20-2a/2 clarifies that we must not intentionally put spin on the ball when we drop it, there's something else to consider. Note that the Rules don't tell us where we must stand in relation to the spot upon which we intend to drop. If you're on a slope you may decide to stand with your feet either higher or lower than the spot where you intend to drop. Consequently you have the option to increase or decrease the height from which the ball will fall in relationship to the ground when it's dropped "from shoulder height" — and therefore the speed at which it will strike the course.

That speed difference can be significant margin depending on the severity of the slope. The more or less distance the ball falls likely means the more or less distance it will bounce, so with the "high-stance vs. low-stance option" you've got a good deal of legal influence you can administer. Of course, this sort of drop control extends to all drops, not just those associated with Water Hazard relief. (By the way, the reason this particular "influence" over the movement of the ball isn't illegal is because Rule 1-2, which otherwise outlaws exerting influence on the movement of the ball, specifically makes an exception for "an action expressly permitted" by another Rule.)

It's pretty darn upsetting if you've already suffered a penalty stroke for going in a Water Hazard and then end up with another unexpected challenge when your ball bounces into a bad location. So it's more than worth the trouble to consider all these issues before you drop.

⚑ ⚑ ⚑

Drop Closer To The Hole

I don't know how many times the words, "not nearer the hole" appear in the *Rules of Golf* when discussing a drop, but it's a lot. So many times in fact that they sometimes create a false general impression with people.

I've seen well-meaning players dutifully pick up their ball when they shouldn't have — for instance after it's bounced slightly closer to the hole than the spot it landed after a 26-1b drop from a Water Hazard. They did this in order to re-drop it, even though it ended up in an attractive position, because they mistakenly thought that the fact that the ball bounced closer to the hole than the point they dropped required them to. (It's certainly true that your ball bouncing closer to the hole than the point where it last crossed the margin of the hazard would require a re-drop, but when you've already moved five yards back for your drop using 26-1b's "no limit to how far behind the water hazard the ball may be dropped" option, a ball then bouncing up to two club-lengths closer to the hole from the point it hit the course remains validly in play.)

☃ ☃ ☃

Segment of Rule:

18-2. By Player, Partner, Caddie or Equipment

Except as permitted by the Rules, when a player's ball is in play, if

i.   the player, his partner or either of their caddies:
  - lifts or moves the ball,
  - touches it purposely (except with a club in the act of addressing the ball), or
  - causes the ball to move, or
ii. the equipment of the player or his partner causes the ball to move, the player incurs a penalty of one stroke.

If the ball is moved, it must be replaced, unless the movement of the ball occurs after the player has begun the stroke or the backward movement of the club for the stroke and the stroke is made.

Rule:

20-2. Dropping and Re-Dropping

c. When to Re-Drop

A dropped ball must be re-dropped, without penalty, if it:

i.   rolls into and comes to rest in a hazard;
ii.   rolls out of and comes to rest outside a hazard;
iii. rolls onto and comes to rest on a putting green;
iv.   rolls and comes to rest out of bounds;
v.   rolls to and comes to rest in a position where there is interference by the condition from which relief was taken under Rule 24-2b (immovable obstruction), Rule 25-1 (abnormal ground conditions), Rule 25-3 (wrong putting green) or a Local Rule (Rule 33-8a), or rolls back into the pitch-mark from which it was lifted under Rule 25-2 (embedded ball);
vi.   rolls and comes to rest more than two club-lengths from where it first struck a part of the course; or
vii. rolls and comes to rest nearer the hole than:
  a. its original position or estimated position (see Rule 20-2b) unless otherwise permitted by the Rules; or
  b. the nearest point of relief or maximum available relief (Rule 24-2, 25-1 or 25-3); or
  c. the point where the original ball last crossed the margin of the *hazard* or lateral water hazard (Rule 26-1).

If the ball when re-dropped rolls into any position listed above, it must be placed as near as possible to the spot where it first struck a part of the course when re-dropped.

Note 1:   If a ball when dropped or re-dropped comes to rest and subsequently moves, the ball must be played as it lies, unless the provisions of any other Rule apply.
Note 2:   If a ball to be re-dropped or placed under this Rule is not immediately recoverable, another ball may be substituted.
(Use of dropping zone - see Appendix I; Part B; Section 8)

Erroneously picking up this ball creates more problems for you. Once that's happened Rule 18-2(i) says you have to replace the ball and take an additional penalty stroke for having inappropriately lifted it when it was in play. Worse, if you don't replace the ball where it was you end up playing from a wrong place resulting in a loss of hole or a two stroke penalty instead (or maybe even worse in Stroke Play if the advantage is deemed a "Serious Breach" as described in the details within Rule 20-7). All for making a mistake caused by confusion while trying to adhere to the Rules. Ouch! It really pays to read and understand Rule 20-2c's list of occasions when a re-drop is required, particularly the (vii) segment discussing the particulars of when the ball bouncing closer to the hole is actually a problem.

ẽ ẽ ẽ

Local Rule:

6. Dropping Zones

The *Committee* may establish dropping zones on which balls may or must be dropped when the *Committee* considers that it is not feasible or practicable to proceed exactly in conformity with Rule 24-2b or Rule 24-3 (Immovable Obstruction), Rule 25-1b or 25-1c (Abnormal Ground Conditions), 25-3 (Wrong Putting Green), Rule 26-1 (Water Hazards and Lateral Water Hazards) or Rule 28 (Ball Unplayable).

Generally, such dropping zones should be provided as an additional relief option to those available under the Rule itself, rather than being mandatory.

Using the example of a dropping zone for a *water hazard*, when such a dropping zone is established, the following Local Rule is recommended:

"If a ball is in or it is known or virtually certain that a ball that has not been found is in the *water hazard* (specify location), the player may:

i.   proceed under Rule 26-1; or

ii. as an additional option, drop a ball, under penalty of one stroke, in the dropping zone.

Penalty For Breach Of Local Rule:
Match play - Loss of hole; Stroke play - Two strokes."

Note: When using a dropping zone the following provisions apply regarding the dropping and re-dropping of the ball:

a.   The player does not have to stand within the dropping zone when dropping the ball.

b.   The dropped ball must first strike a part of the *course* within the dropping zone.

c.   If the dropping zone is defined by a line, the line is within the dropping zone.

d.   The dropped ball does not have to come to rest within the dropping zone.

e.   The dropped ball must be re-dropped if it rolls and comes to rest in a position covered by Rule 20-2c(i-vi).

f.   The dropped ball may roll nearer the *hole* than the spot where it first struck a part of the *course*, provided it comes to rest within two club-lengths of that spot and not into any of the positions covered by (e).

g.   Subject to the provisions of (e) and (f), the dropped ball may roll and come to rest nearer the *hole* than:
   - its original position or estimated position (see Rule 20-2b);
   - the *nearest point of relief* or maximum available relief (Rule 24-2, 25-1 or 25-3); or
   - the point where the original ball last crossed the margin of the *water hazard* or *lateral water hazard* (Rule 26-1)

℞ ℞ ℞

Beyond this mistaken view of a dropped ball bouncing closer to the hole than the point it hits the course, there are occasions when you actually are allowed to initially drop closer to the hole than the point where your last shot stopped: When a Dropping Zone is an option. Dropping Zones may be created via Local Rule for a variety of reasons, and a Water Hazard is just one of them. Relief from Immovable Obstructions (Rule 24-2), Abnormal Ground Conditions (Rule 25-1), Wrong Putting Green (Rule 25-3), Ball Unplayable (Rule 28) and Temporary Immovable Obstructions are all valid reasons for a Committee to create a Dropping Zone. The Zone might very well be closer to the hole than where your ball previously came to rest, so on those occasions your drop point (not just the position the ball rolls to) can legally be closer to the hole.

℞

There's one last detail to keep in mind. In Appendix 1, part A, section 6, the Local Rule regarding the use of Dropping Zones is described, including the provisions on their use. Provision (d) points out that a ball dropped in a Dropping Zone does not have to stay within the Zone to be a valid drop, and even more to the point provision (g) explicitly tells us that the ball may legally end up nearer the hole than its original position, the Nearest Point of Relief or the point where the ball last crossed the margin of a Water Hazard. So the bottom line is that the Dropping Zone may be closer to the hole than the point from which you were getting relief, and if you drop the ball in the Zone but it bounces outside the Zone closer to the hole it's still validly in play as long as some other situation didn't arise (such as the ball bouncing more than two club-lengths away from the point it hit the Zone).

Sometimes a Committee's Local Rule might demand that you not use a Zone that's closer to the hole, but if it doesn't, you might very well benefit from that advantage.

Decisions:

18-2/12 Player Entitled to Relief from Condition Lifts Ball; Player Then Replaces Ball and Plays It from Original Position

Q. A player elects to take relief from an immovable obstruction or abnormal ground condition and lifts his ball. He then realizes that the only area in which he may drop under the Rules is such that his ball, when dropped, will almost certainly be unplayable. He replaces his ball and plays it from its original position. What is the ruling?

A. The player was entitled to lift the ball to take relief under Rule 24 or 25. However, by subsequently deciding not to take relief, his right to lift the ball was negated and he incurred a penalty stroke under Rule 18-2 for having lifted his ball in play.

18-2/12.5 Player Entitled to Relief Without Penalty from Condition Lifts Ball; Chooses Not to Take Relief and Wishes to Proceed Under the Unplayable Ball Rule

Q. A player elects to take relief from an immovable obstruction or abnormal ground condition and lifts his ball. He then realizes that the only area in which he may drop under the Rules is such that his ball, when dropped, will almost certainly be unplayable. May the player deem the ball unplayable and proceed under Rule 28?

A. Yes. The player has the following options:

1. replace the ball in its original position under penalty of one stroke (Rule 18-2) and then proceed under Rule 28, incurring an additional penalty of one stroke; or
2. proceed directly under Rule 28b or c, without replacing the ball and using the spot where the ball originally lay as the reference point for the relief procedure, incurring a penalty stroke under Rule 28 and an additional penalty stroke under Rule 18-2; or
3. drop the ball in accordance with Rule 24 or 25 and then, using its new position as a reference point, proceed under Rule 28incurring a penalty of one stroke; or
4. proceed directly under Rule 28a, without dropping the ball in accordance with Rule 24 or 25, incurring a penalty of one stroke under Rule 28 and no penalty under Rule 18-2, as he does not need to establish a new reference point before proceeding under Rule 28a.

⚐ ⚐ ⚐

Determine What Free Relief Might Cost You

While I'm on the topic of drops I want to give a bit of advice that's always worth heeding: Never pick up your ball to take a free drop before you're convinced that the place you'll be permitted to drop it is better than the spot upon which your ball is currently sitting. Immovable Obstructions, Casual Water, Ground Under Repair; they all provide you with the option of free relief. Some players impulsively decide to take that relief before they analyze exactly where they'll have to drop, and that can end up being a big problem.

Let's focus on the Immovable Obstruction of a paved cart path. Once you pick up your ball with the intention of getting free relief, you only have three choices: drop it in the place that's prescribed by Rule 24-2 (within one club-length of the Nearest Point of Relief and no closer to the hole), put it back down on the cart path — at the cost of a penalty stroke under Rule 18-2(i) for having inappropriately lifted your ball, or take an Unplayable Ball penalty under Rule 28. Clearly, it's worthwhile considering whether the first, "free" choice is really going to work for you before you commit.

Sometimes the place "within one club-length of the Nearest Point of Relief and no closer to the hole" will be in high grass. Sometimes it will be in a bush. Or on the roots of a tree. Would that be better than hitting off the cart path to begin with? Maybe not, think about it before you begin!

It's even possible that after picking up your ball from a cart path you *will not even be physically able to drop* within one club-length of the Nearest Point of Relief. If you imagine your ball stopping at the edge of a paved cart path that's butted up against a sheer rock face or the trunk of a massive tree, you'll see what I mean. The Nearest Point of Relief from the cart path (and the associated club-length) might very well be within the outcrop or the tree's trunk! If you can't drop in the prescribed area of the Nearest Point of Relief, you can't drop for free at all — you will either have to replace your ball back on the edge of the path at the cost of a penalty stroke — a complete waste — or take an Unplayable Ball penalty at the cost of either <u>two</u> strokes (Rule 18-2 penalty stroke plus Rule 28 penalty stroke) or a Rule 28 Stroke and Distance penalty. Decisions 18-2/12 and 18-2/12.5 describe these expensive options in painful detail, and analyzing them makes it clear that in some cases you would have been much better off either hitting from the cart path (perhaps even putting if you're afraid of injury) or deciding to take an Unplayable Ball penalty prior to picking up your ball, in which cases either no penalty stroke or just a single penalty stroke might have accomplished something useful for you.

☙ ☙ ☙

Decisions:

24-2b/3.5 Player Unable Physically to Determine Nearest Point of Relief

Q. In proceeding under Rule 24-2b(i) or Rule 25-1b(i), the Definition of "Nearest Point of Relief" provides that to determine the nearest point of relief accurately, the player should use the club, address position, direction of play and swing (right or left-handed) that he would have used from the original position had the obstruction or condition not been there. What is the procedure if a player is unable physically to determine the nearest point of relief because, for example, that point is within the trunk of a tree or a boundary fence prevents the player from adopting the required address position?

A. The nearest point of relief in both cases must be estimated and the player must drop the ball within one club-length of the estimated point, not nearer the hole.

24-2b/3.7 Diagram Illustrating Player Unable to Determine Nearest Point of Relief

The diagram illustrates the point raised in Decision 24-2b/3.5 where a player may be unable to determine the nearest point of relief from an immovable obstruction and will need to estimate this point under Rule 24-2b.

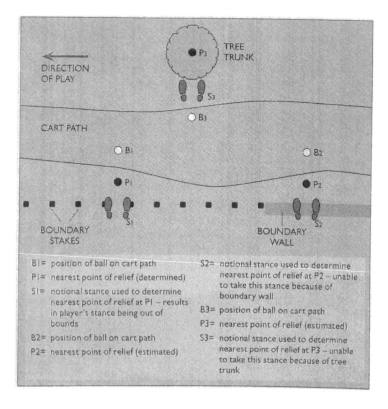

B1 = position of ball on cart path

P1 = nearest point of relief (determined)

S1 = notional stance used to determine nearest point of relief at P1 – results in player's stance being out of bounds

B2 = position of ball on cart path

P2 = nearest point of relief (estimated)

S2 = notional stance used to determine nearest point of relief at P2 – unable to take this stance because of boundary wall

B3 = position of ball on cart path

P3 = nearest point of relief (estimated)

S3 = notional stance used to determine nearest point of relief at P3 – unable to take this stance because of tree trunk

🍂 🍂 🍂

1-4/8.5 Nearest Point of Relief from Cart Path Is in Casual Water, Nearest Point of Relief from Casual Water Is Back on Cart Path; Impracticable for Player to Drop Ball Into Area of Casual Water

Q. In the circumstances described in Decision 1-4/8, if the nature of the area of casual water were such that it was impracticable or impossible for the player to drop the ball, when taking relief from the cart path, into the area of casual water, how may the player proceed?

A. If it is impracticable for the player to proceed under one of the two Rules, he may, in equity (Rule 1-4), obtain relief without penalty as follows: Using the position of the ball on the cart path, the nearest point of relief from both the cart path and the casual water must be determined that is not in a hazard or on a putting green. The player must lift the ball and drop it within one club-length of and not nearer the hole than the nearest point of relief, on a part of the course that avoids interference by the cart path and the casual water and is not in a hazard or on a putting green.

It would be considered impracticable for the player to drop the ball in the area of casual water if the casual water were so deep that unreasonable effort would be required to retrieve a ball lying in this area of casual water - see Decision 25-1/1.

Other examples of conditions into which it would be considered impracticable for the player to drop the ball would include:

- in or under an immovable obstruction such that it would be extremely difficult or impossible to drop the ball (e.g., inside a locked building or beneath a rain-shelter that is raised off the ground).
- within a large hole made by a greenkeeper or similar area of ground under repair from which the player could not reasonably be expected to play a ball.

Since boundary walls and fences are excluded from the definition of Immovable Obstructions, they can cause a similar problem to that which I referred to with the rock outcrop — this time perhaps preventing you from taking a stance rather than taking a drop. Decisions 24-2b/3.5 and 24-2b/3.7 provide guidance and diagrams regarding estimating the Nearest Point of Relief for these difficult drops. On the positive side, I should point out that if a separate Immovable Obstruction like a locked building on the course is at the edge of a cart path (something other than a natural object like a rock face or tree) Decision 1-4/8.5 might give you an attractive drop option.

Rule:

Rule 18 - Ball at Rest Moved
18-1. By Outside Agency
If a ball at rest is moved by an outside agency, there is no penalty and the ball must be replaced.

Note: It is a question of fact whether a ball has been moved by an outside agency. In order to apply this Rule, it must be known or virtually certain that an outside agency has moved the ball. In the absence of such knowledge or certainty, the player must play the ball as it lies or, if the ball is not found, proceed under Rule 27-1.

(Player's ball at rest moved by another ball - see Rule 18-5)

Note 1 at end of Rule 18:

Note 1:   If a ball to be replaced under this Rule is not immediately recoverable, another ball may be substituted.

Decision:

26-1/1 Meaning of "Known or Virtually Certain"
When a ball has been struck towards a water hazard and cannot be found, a player may not assume that his ball is in the water hazard simply because there is a possibility that the ball may be in the water hazard. In order to proceed under Rule 26-1, it must be "known or virtually certain" that the ball is in the water hazard. In the absence of "knowledge or virtual certainty" that it lies in a water hazard, a ball that cannot be found must be considered lost somewhere other than in a water hazard and the player must proceed under Rule 27-1.

When a player's ball cannot be found, "knowledge" may be gained that his ball is in a water hazard in a number of ways. The player or his caddie or other members of his match or group may actually observe the ball disappear into the water hazard. Evidence provided by other reliable witnesses may also establish that the ball is in the water hazard. Such evidence could come from a referee, an observer, spectators or other outside agencies. It is important that all readily accessible information be considered because, for example, the mere fact that a ball has splashed in a water hazard would not always provide "knowledge" that the ball is in the water hazard, as there are instances when a ball may skip out of, and come to rest outside, the hazard.

In the absence of "knowledge" that the ball is in the water hazard, Rule 26-1 requires there to be "virtual certainty" that the player's ball is in the water hazard in order to proceed under this Rule. Unlike "knowledge," "virtual certainty" implies some small degree of doubt about the actual location of a ball that has not been found. However, "virtual certainty" also means that, although the ball has not been found, when all readily available information is considered, the conclusion that there is nowhere that the ball could be except in the water hazard would be justified.

In determining whether "virtual certainty" exists, some of the relevant factors in the area of the water hazard to be considered include topography, turf conditions, grass heights, visibility, weather conditions and the proximity of trees, bushes and abnormal ground conditions.

The same principles would apply for a ball that may have been moved by an outside agency (Rule 18-1) or a ball that has not been found and may be in an obstruction (Rule 24-3) or an abnormal ground condition (Rule 25-1c).

Rule:

20-3. Placing and Replacing
c. Spot Not Determinable
If it is impossible to determine the spot where the ball is to be placed or replaced:

i.   through the green , the ball must be dropped as near as possible to the place where it lay but not in a hazard or on a putting green;
ii. in a hazard, the ball must be dropped in the hazard as near as possible to the place where it lay;
iii. on the putting green, the ball must be placed as near as possible to the place where it lay but not in a hazard.

Exception: When resuming play (Rule 6-8d), if the spot where the ball is to be placed is impossible to determine, it must be estimated and the ball placed on the estimated spot.

Decision:

18-1/5 Ball Stolen by Outside Agency from Unknown Spot
Q. At a par-3 hole, part of the green and the adjoining area cannot be seen from the tee. In this unseen area are a bunker, fairway and a dry water hazard.
A player plays towards this obscured area and cannot tell where the ball comes to rest. When the players are near the green, they see a boy running away with a ball in his hand. The boy throws the ball back and the player identifies it as his ball.
The player is unable to determine from where to play his next stroke under Rule 18-1. He does not know whether the ball was on the green, on the fairway or in one of the hazards. How should he proceed?
A. As it was impossible to know where the ball should have been replaced under Rule 18-1, the player should, in equity (Rule 1-4), drop the ball in an area which was neither the most, nor the least, favorable of the various areas where it was equally possible that the ball originally lay.

Get A Reprieve For A Lost Ball

Typically, if you can't find your ball within five minutes after you've begun your search, you're out of luck — you're saddled with a Stroke and Distance penalty and forced to take the "walk of shame" back to the spot from which you last hit (unless of course you hit a Provisional Ball). But sometimes there's a better option for the Rules-wise. In the details of the following three Rules, you'll find something very helpful: Rule 18, Ball at Rest Moved; Rule 24, Obstructions; and Rule 25-1, Abnormal Ground Conditions.

Ⓟ

Let's take a closer look, starting with Rule 18-1. Here we see that if your ball at rest is moved by an Outside Agency, such as a random person playing a parallel hole on the course or a Fellow Competitor in a Stroke Play event, it must be replaced, penalty-free. In order to apply this Rule, you must know or be Virtually Certain that your ball was in fact moved by an Outside Agency, so you have to first consider the precise meaning of those words as described in Decision 26-1/1. If you pass that test, you're good to go, even if a thief (human, bird, dog, fox, snake) has purposely taken your ball and you will never see it again. Note 1 at the end of Rule 18 tells us that if we can't immediately recover our ball we may substitute one. And Rule 20-3c tells us where to drop or place our substituted ball if we don't know exactly where it came to rest. Decision 18-1/5 even offers direction as to what to do if your ball is stolen by an Outside Agency from a completely unknown spot. There are a few hurdles here, I know, but it's nevertheless possible to get freedom from the trauma of a Stroke and Distance penalty if you make it over those hurdles. It's a feat that's been happily accomplished by players at the highest level of the game (and under the most intense scrutiny) whose balls have been stolen.

Rule:

24-3. Ball in Obstruction Not Found

It is a question of fact whether a ball that has not been found after having been struck toward an obstruction is in the obstruction. In order to apply this Rule, it must be known or virtually certain that the ball is in the obstruction. In the absence of such knowledge or certainty, the player must proceed under Rule 27-1.

a. Ball in Movable Obstruction Not Found

If it is known or virtually certain that a ball that has not been found is in a movable obstruction, the player may substitute another ball and take relief, without penalty, under this Rule. If he elects to do so, he must remove the obstruction and through the green or in a hazard drop a ball, or on the putting green place a ball, as near as possible to the spot directly under the place where the ball last crossed the outermost limits of the movable obstruction, but not nearer the hole.

b. Ball in Immovable Obstruction Not Found

If it is known or virtually certain that a ball that has not been found is in an immovable obstruction, the player may take relief under this Rule. If he elects to do so, the spot where the ball last crossed the outermost limits of the obstruction must be determined and, for the purpose of applying this Rule, the ball is deemed to lie at this spot and the player must proceed as follows:

i.   THROUGH THE GREEN: If the ball last crossed the outermost limits of the immovable obstruction at a spot through the green, the player may substitute another ball, without penalty, and take relief as prescribed in Rule 24-2b(i).

ii. IN A BUNKER: If the ball last crossed the outermost limits of the immovable obstruction at a spot in a bunker, the player may substitute another ball, without penalty, and take relief as prescribed in Rule 24-2b(ii).

iii. IN A WATER HAZARD (INCLUDING A LATERAL WATER HAZARD): If the ball last crossed the outermost limits of the immovable obstruction at a spot in a water hazard, the player is not entitled to relief without penalty. The player must proceed under Rule 26-1.

iv. ON THE PUTTING GREEN: If the ball last crossed the outermost limits of the immovable obstruction at a spot on the putting green, the player may substitute another ball, without penalty, and take relief as prescribed in Rule 24-2b(iii).

Sparing ourselves the thief-related drama for a moment, let's move on to Rule 24-3, which covers what to do when a ball in an Obstruction isn't found. Lose your ball in an Immovable Obstruction like a maintenance shed, parking lot full of cars, or a dumpster? No problem, as long as the artificial construction is in bounds and the place the ball last crossed the outermost limits of the Immovable Obstruction is not in a Water Hazard. As long as you know or are Virtually Certain it's stayed in the Obstruction, you're good to go. In this case, Rule 24-3a tells you where to drop or place if it's a Movable Obstruction, and 24-3b guides you if it's an Immovable Obstruction.

Rule:

25-1. Abnormal Ground Conditions

c. Ball in Abnormal Ground Condition Not Found

It is a question of fact whether a ball that has not been found after having been struck toward an abnormal ground condition is in such a condition. In order to apply this Rule, it must be known or virtually certain that the ball is in the abnormal ground condition. In the absence of such knowledge or certainty, the player must proceed under Rule 27-1.

If it is known or virtually certain that a ball that has not been found is in an abnormal ground condition, the player may take relief under this Rule. If he elects to do so, the spot where the ball last crossed the outermost limits of the abnormal ground condition must be determined and, for the purpose of applying this Rule, the ball is deemed to lie at this spot and the player must proceed as follows:

i. THROUGH THE GREEN: If the ball last crossed the outermost limits of the abnormal ground condition at a spot through the green, the player may substitute another ball, without penalty, and take relief as prescribed in Rule 25-1b(i).

ii. IN A BUNKER: If the ball last crossed the outermost limits of the abnormal ground condition at a spot in a bunker, the player may substitute another ball, without penalty, and take relief as prescribed in Rule 25-1b(ii).

iii. IN A WATER HAZARD (INCLUDING A LATERAL WATER HAZARD): If the ball last crossed the outermost limits of the abnormal ground condition at a spot in a water hazard, the player is not entitled to relief without penalty. The player must proceed under Rule 26-1.

iv. ON THE PUTTING GREEN: If the ball last crossed the outermost limits of the abnormal ground condition at a spot on the putting green, the player may substitute another ball, without penalty, and take relief as prescribed in Rule 25-1b(iii).

Decision:

24-2b/16 Obstruction Interferes But Ball Unplayable Due to Some Other Condition

Q. A player's ball lies between two exposed tree roots. The ball is clearly unplayable due to the roots. An immovable obstruction is so located that it would interfere with the player's backswing if the player could play the ball. The player claims he is entitled to relief, without penalty, under Rule 24-2b(i). Is the player correct?

A. No. See Exception under Rule 24-2b. The player must invoke Rule 28.

♜ ♜ ♜

Rule 25-1, Abnormal Ground Conditions, is the last chapter in my Lost Ball Tale of Salvation. As with a ball moved by an Outside Agency or lost in an Obstruction, you must know or be Virtually Certain the ball is lost in the condition to get free relief. But if you do know or are Virtually Certain your ball that was lost in Casual Water; Ground Under Repair; or hole, cast or runway made by a burrowing animal, a reptile or a bird — it can be substituted for by dropping or placing under the guidance of 25-1c. And don't forget that Ground Under Repair includes material piled for removal by a greenkeeper, even if it's not marked. So next fall when your ball ends up lost in a huge pile of leaves temporarily blown to the side of the fairway, you might regret having lost a nice ball, but you don't have to regret a Stroke and Distance penalty too.

Fight Injustice

It should be noted that the Rules are pretty generous in terms of allowing free relief from Movable Obstructions and Abnormal Ground Conditions. But being generous doesn't mean they are complete push-overs, and you shouldn't be either if an Opponent or Fellow Competitor inappropriately tries to take advantage of one of these Rules. There is an Exception noted in the relief segment of both Rule 24-2 and Rule 25-1:

Exception: A player may not take relief under this Rule if (a) interference by anything other than an immovable obstruction makes the stroke clearly impracticable or (b) interference by an immovable obstruction would occur only through use of a clearly unreasonable stroke or an unnecessarily abnormal stance, swing or direction of play.

The same Exception wording applies to Abnormal Ground Conditions, just switch out those words for "immovable obstruction."

The first thing to do when contemplating this issue (and I only mean this half in jest) is to look up the definition of "impracticable." For our purposes, it essentially means almost impossible. So if your Opponent or Fellow Competitor has his ball roll into a hole in the trunk of a tree where he pretty much can't even get a clubhead on it, but there is a paved cart path that he'd be standing on if he were to try, there is, as Jerry Seinfeld's neighborhood restaurateur used to say, "No soup for you." Your Opponent or Fellow Competitor has no right to free relief in that situation. If he complains, refer him to Decision 24-2b/16 which makes your position crystal clear.

Decisions:

24-2b/17 Obstruction Interferes with Abnormal Stroke; Abnormal Stroke Reasonable in Circumstances

Q. A right-handed player's ball is so close to a boundary fence on the left of a hole that the player, in order to play towards the hole, must play left-handed. In making a left-handed stroke, the player's backswing would be interfered with by an immovable obstruction. Is the player entitled to relief from the obstruction?

A. The player is entitled to relief since use of an abnormal (left-handed) stroke is reasonable in the circumstances - see Exception under Rule 24-2b.

The proper procedure is for the player to take relief for a left-handed stroke in accordance with Rule 24-2b(i).

The player may then use a normal right-handed swing for his next stroke. If the obstruction interferes with the swing or stance for the right-handed stroke, the player may take relief for the right-handed stroke in accordance with Rule 24-2b(i).

24-2b/18 Obstruction Interferes with Abnormal Stroke; Abnormal Stroke Not Reasonable in Circumstances

Q. A right-handed player's ball is in a poor lie. A nearby immovable obstruction would not interfere with a normal right-handed swing but it would interfere with a left-handed swing. The player says he wishes to make his next stroke left-handed and, since the obstruction would interfere with such a stroke, he is entitled to proceed under Rule 24-2b. May the player invoke Rule 24-2b?

A. No. If the only reason for the player to use a left-handed stroke is to escape a poor lie, use of an abnormal (left-handed) stroke is clearly unreasonable and the player is not entitled to invoke Rule 24-2b - see Exception under Rule 24-2b.

⚑ ⚑ ⚑

Don't forget that the exception and its associated prohibition covers unnecessarily abnormal stances and clearly unreasonable swings too, so if a player is unjustifiably spreading his legs to their widest extent to get a toe on a sprinkler head, that action is not "soup-worthy" either. Play it as it lies, dude. You might want to note that this sort of restriction on a free drop even applies to the Local Rule allowing relief from an Embedded Ball anywhere Through the Green — it's possible to have a ball embed in an area from which it's otherwise impracticable to strike it.

A word to the wise, egg on your face is not a good look. So before you get completely carried away trying to refuse all sorts of free relief, do please give a read through Decision 24-2b/17, which describes how an abnormal stroke might in fact be reasonable in certain conditions, and 24-2b/18 which describes when it's not.

Rule:

2-5. Doubt as to Procedure; Disputes and Claims

In match play, if a doubt or dispute arises between the players, a player may make a claim. If no duly authorized representative of the Committee is available within a reasonable time, the players must continue the match without delay. The Committee may consider a claim only if it has been made in a timely manner and if the player making the claim has notified his opponent at the time (i) that he is making a claim or wants a ruling and (ii) of the facts upon which the claim or ruling is to be based.

A claim is considered to have been made in a timely manner if, upon discovery of circumstances giving rise to a claim, the player makes his claim (i) before any player in the match plays from the next teeing ground, or (ii) in the case of the last hole of the match, before all players in the match leave the putting green, or (iii) when the circumstances giving rise to the claim are discovered after all the players in the match have left the putting green of the final hole, before the result of the match has been officially announced.

A claim relating to a prior hole in the match may only be considered by the Committee if it is based on facts previously unknown to the player making the claim and he had been given wrong information (Rules 6-2a or 9) by an opponent. Such a claim must be made in a timely manner.

Once the result of the match has been officially announced, a claim may not be considered by the Committee, unless it is satisfied that (i) the claim is based on facts which were previously unknown to the player making the claim at the time the result was officially announced, (ii) the player making the claim had been given wrong information by an opponent and (iii) the opponent knew he was giving wrong information. There is no time limit on considering such a claim.

Note 1:   A player may disregard a breach of the Rules by his opponent provided there is no agreement by the sides to waive a Rule (Rule 1-3).

Note 2:   In match play, if a player is doubtful of his rights or the correct procedure, he may not complete the play of the hole with two balls.

ళ ళ ళ

Decisions:

2-5/8.5 Player and Opponent Agree on Incorrect Procedure; Whether Valid Claim May Be Made After Procedure Followed

Q. In a match, a player's ball comes to rest on an artificially-surfaced road. He is uncertain if the road is to be treated as an immovable obstruction or an integral part of the course. He asks his opponent and they agree that the player should treat the road as an immovable obstruction. The player drops the ball in accordance with the procedure under Rule 24-2b and plays it. Prior to playing from the next tee, the opponent discovers that he and the player were wrong as the Committee had introduced a Local Rule declaring the road to be an integral part of the course and, therefore, the player was not entitled to take relief under Rule 24-2b. The player should have incurred a loss of hole penalty under Rule 18 for lifting his ball without authority and failing to replace it. May the opponent claim the hole?

A. No. The claim must not be considered by the Committee because the opponent and the player agreed that the player was entitled to relief under Rule 24-2b. When this agreement was reached, there was no longer a doubtful or disputed point and there was no basis under Rule 2-5 for making a claim.
   The players were not in breach of Rule 1-3 as they believed at the time they were proceeding properly.

2-5/2 Procedure for a Valid Claim

For a claim to be valid, the claimant must notify his opponent (i) that he is making a claim or wants a ruling and, (ii) the facts of the situation. He must do so within the time required by Rule 2-5. For example, Rule 16-1e prohibits putting from a stance astride an extension of the line of putt behind the ball. In a match between A and B, if A putts from a stance astride an extension of the line and B states "that is not allowed, you are penalized" or "I'm making a claim because of that stroke," the Committee should consider the claim.

Statements by B such as "I'm not sure that's allowed" or "I don't think you can do that" do not by themselves constitute a valid claim because each statement does not contain the notice of a claim or that he wants a ruling and the facts of the situation.

༺ ༻ ༼

Know What To Do When You Don't Know What To Do

Sooner or later everyone gets confused about what the right ruling might be. When it happens to you out there on the course, you don't have to be like Tennessee Williams's Blanche DuBois and always depend on the kindness of strangers. (Your stranger might be wrong!)

Don't worry, the Rules can be of help to you even if you don't know them. How do you take advantage of that oxymoron? Look to Rule 2-5 if you're playing Match Play, or Rule 3-3 if you're playing Stroke.

In a Match, if you and your Opponent(s) are confused about a Rule, you have the option of agreeing to a resolution, even if it's incorrect as far as the Rules go, as long as you don't intentionally agree to waive a Rule or a penalty that you know exists. Decision 2-5/8.5 confirms that the resolution to which you agree becomes "law" for the purposes of that occasion. In this way the Rules start out supportive of the ignorant, but that's not the end of how they help resolve conflicts.

Rule 2-5 makes it clear that an Opponent has very specific obligations, all of which must be met, if he wishes to successfully contest an action that a player takes. The obligations consist of the Opponent making his claim in a "timely" manner by notifying the player ("timely" is defined in the Rule), the Opponent must also notify the player of the facts of the situation upon which his claim is based, and of course the Opponent must end up being proved right in his assertion. Decision 2-5/2 describes the procedure in more detail, but in any case if you're the challenged player there are several loopholes through which you might squeeze. And even if you're not completely sure how a Rule applies to your situation, knowing the obligations your Opponent must bear in order to prevail and making sure he actually fulfills them can end up giving you an out even if you're wrong.

ཏ ཏ ཏ

Rule:

3-3. Doubt as to Procedure
a. Procedure for Competitor

In stroke play only, if a competitor is doubtful of his rights or the correct procedure during the play of a hole, he may, without penalty, complete the hole with two balls. To proceed under this Rule, he must decide to play two balls after the doubtful situation has arisen and before taking further action (e.g., making a stroke at the original ball).

The competitor should announce to his marker or a fellow-competitor:
- that he intends to play two balls; and
- which ball he wishes to count if the Rules permit the procedure used for that ball.

Before returning his score card, the competitor must report the facts of the situation to the Committee. If he fails to do so, he is disqualified.

If the competitor has taken further action before deciding to play two balls, he has not proceeded under Rule 3-3 and the score with the original ball counts. The competitor incurs no penalty for playing the second ball.

In Stroke Play, dealing with confusion regarding the Rules is entirely different. But you can still help yourself if you don't know how the Rules demand you deal with a situation, and since Stroke Play scoring errors can easily lead to disqualification (instead of the typical loss of a hole in Match Play), it's even more important that you deal with Rules confusion the right way.

Rule 3-3a, Stroke Play's Doubt as to Procedure, tells you what you do. You should read it thoroughly, (as well as the next segment, "b. Committee Determination of Score for Hole") but the shorthand is that when you find yourself in a questionable situation, instead of guessing the right procedure and before you take any further action, you should announce to your Marker or Fellow Competitor your intention to play two balls. And state which of the two balls you'd like to have count toward your score if the Rules permit. Then you get to play a ball in the way you hope you'll be allowed as well as one in the way you fear you must. Be aware that you cannot play more than two balls in this situation, even if you are unsure about the legality of either of your two choices — there's a limit to the Rules' benevolence here. And last, be sure that at the conclusion of your round you report the facts of your actions to the Committee — even if your score is identical for each of the two balls. If you fail to have that discussion, you will be disqualified.

One more tip, when you describe your trials and tribulations to the Committee, don't call your second ball a "Provisional" ball, it's not! It's a "second ball" and calling it a Provisional might confuse things. And in any case, your second ball deserves to be called by its proper name, you've already caused everyone enough grief.

Rule:

Rule 21 - Cleaning Ball

A ball on the putting green may be cleaned when lifted under Rule 16-1b. Elsewhere, a ball may be cleaned when lifted, except when it has been lifted:

a. To determine if it is unfit for play (Rule 5-3);
b. For identification (Rule 12-2), in which case it may be cleaned only to the extent necessary for identification; or
c. Because it is assisting or interfering with play (Rule 22).

If a player cleans his ball during play of a hole except as provided in this Rule, he incurs a penalty of one stroke and the ball, if lifted, must be replaced.

If a player who is required to replace a ball fails to do so, he incurs the general penalty under the applicable Rule, but there is no additional penalty under Rule 21.

Exception: If a player incurs a penalty for failing to act in accordance with Rule 5-3, 12-2 or 22, there is no additional penalty under Rule 21.

Decisions:

25/1 Soft, Mushy Earth

Q. Is soft, mushy earth casual water?
A. No. Soft, mushy earth is not casual water unless water is visible on the surface before or after the player takes his stance - see Definition of "Casual Water."

33-2a/2 Declaring Area as Ground Under Repair During Competition Round

Q. A's ball is in a poor lie in a washed-out area which warrants being marked as ground under repair but is not so marked. He deems the ball unplayable and proceeds under Rule 28, incurring a one-stroke penalty.
Subsequently, in the same competition round, B's ball is in the same area. B requests the Committee to declare the area ground under repair. Would the Committee be justified in declaring the area ground under repair in such circumstances?
A. Yes; this applies in either match or stroke play. However, it is preferable that all areas which warrant marking as ground under repair should be so marked before the start of a competition.

꙰ ꙰ ꙰

Segment of Rule:

25-1. Abnormal Ground Conditions
b. Relief

Except when the ball is in a water hazard or a lateral water hazard, a player may take relief from interference by an abnormal ground condition as follows:

i.   THROUGH THE GREEN: If the ball lies through the green, the player must lift the ball and drop it, without penalty, within one club-length of and not nearer the hole than the nearest point of relief. The nearest point of relief must not be in a hazard or on a putting green. When the ball is dropped within one club-length of the nearest point of relief, the ball must first strike a part of the course at a spot that avoids interference by the condition and is not in a hazard and not on a putting green.
    The ball may be cleaned when lifted under Rule 25-1b.

Decisions:

3-3/13 Competitor Invokes Rule 3-3; Lifts and Drops Original Ball

Q.   A competitor's ball comes to rest in an area that he feels should be marked as ground under repair. Believing the Committee might declare the area to be ground under repair, he announces that he will invoke Rule 3-3 and play a second ball in accordance with Rule 25-1b and that he wishes his score with the ball played under Rule 25-1b to count if the Rules permit. He marks the position of and lifts the original ball, drops it in accordance with Rule 25-1b and plays it. He then places a second ball where the original lay and plays it. Is the competitor's procedure correct?

A.   Yes. Rule 3-3 does not require the original ball to be played as it lies and, therefore, the competitor's procedure was acceptable. However, it would also have been correct for the competitor to play his original ball as it lay and play a second ball in accordance with Rule 25-1b.

21/5 Player Lifts Ball Under Rule Not Permitting Cleaning and Rotates It When Replaced

Q.   A piece of mud adheres to a player's ball. The player lifts the ball under a Rule which does not permit cleaning. When he replaces the ball, may he place it facing another direction so that the mud would not interfere between the clubface and the ball?

A.   Yes, provided the ball is replaced on the spot from which it was lifted. However, if the player rotated the ball in such a way so as to "tee" it on the mud, he would be in breach of Rule 20-3a.

☙ ☙ ☙

Clean An "Uncleanable" Ball

Rule 21 tells you the specific circumstances in which you're allowed to clean your ball, and of course unless you're on the green most times you're not allowed. Here's a quirky observation related to the preceding Rule 3-3 that can in a rare instance give you an edge. It's a bit esoteric, but if you're of a mind read on.

You're in a Stroke Play event, and you've just hit your ball off line into a muddy area in the rough, and you can see a large glob of mud stuck to it. The unmarked area has no visible water, but nevertheless it's one that potentially could be defined as Ground Under Repair. (Decision 25/1 tells us that soft, mushy earth in itself is not Casual Water, so there's no free relief on that basis.) Decision 33-2a/2 tells us that the Committee may redefine an unmarked area as Ground Under Repair at any time, even during a competition. There's no Committee member around, and you're not sure if you will be granted relief from Ground Under Repair, so you announce to your Fellow Competitor that you're going to play a ball from this unattractive ground as well as a second ball under Rule 3-3, and if the Rules later permit, you want the ball you are about to drop outside of what you believe might be Ground Under Repair to be the one to count.

You reach down and mark your original ball that's in the mud, deciding to use that original ball as the one you will drop under the relief procedure of Rule 25-1 b (i), Abnormal Ground Conditions. You note that this Rule also allows you to clean the ball when lifted, so you wipe that big glob off the ball, drop it on some nice ground and play it. Then you reach into your bag and take another clean ball out and replace it on the spot you marked within the muddy area. Decision 3-3/13 makes it abundantly clear that you had the right to choose which ball you would play from which position, so you have legally worked things out in such a way that you were able to play two completely clean balls. Even if the Committee later rules that the area in question should not be considered Ground Under Repair when you later call the incident to their attention, you at least got to play that shot with a pristine ball.

As I said, it's esoteric, but this particular magic trick shows how intricately the Rules fit together — in this case protecting your right to play the specific ball you prefer and your desire to accommodate the Rules even when you're unsure what a ruling might be.

While on the topic of finding mud on a ball, there's another situation you might want to be aware of even though "cleaning" is not permitted. Decision 21/5 describes a quirky opportunity you have to reorient the mud on your ball even when you're not allowed to clean it off — such as when you lift it for identification.

Get Yourself Between A Drop And A Hard Place

This may surprise you, but there are a number of circumstances in which you might want to drop on a paved cart path. In fact, there are instances where you are required to.

It's worth noting that when taking relief from a Water Hazard, Abnormal Ground Condition, or Unplayable Ball, while the Rules precisely specify where you may drop they don't exclude or prohibit your dropping on an Immovable Obstruction if that Obstruction is within the relief area described. It's also true that if you're taking relief from one Immovable Obstruction (like a building) you may have to drop on a different Immovable Obstruction that's nearby (such as a paved cart path) if that is where the nearest point of relief (and associated club-length) from the initial Obstruction leave you.

As another example, if there's a paved cart path next to a Lateral Water Hazard, and you wish to take relief within two club-lengths of the point where your ball last crossed the hazard margin, and that area is a paved cart path; that's where you must drop. The fact that you may subsequently be provided with the option to take free relief from the cart path in no way cancels your obligation to drop upon it first.

While it may be cumbersome to drop on a paved cart path since the ball typically bounces far (and will likely require a re-drop and then a place according to Rule 20-2c), and while it's likely that you'll want to take relief from the path if your ball stays on it, the reality of the situation is that the repetitive process very nicely gives you two bites at the apple. You can choose to play from the cart path, or choose to take relief once again if it pleases you. That optional combination can easily end up getting you much further away from your original lie than would ordinarily be prescribed — perhaps that's a benefit. And like the "high stance" drop option discussed in the "Navigate Water Hazards" segment above, getting to drop on even a sliver of cart path that may be in range is a legal way to cause your ball to bounce with great vigor, sometimes useful in getting it to go where you want it to go.

The one thing you must always remain aware of is that an Immovable Obstruction like a paved cart path is a valid drop location. If you avoid it, you might very well be dropping in a wrong place and subject to a loss of hole penalty in Match Play or a two-stroke penalty (or worse) in Stroke Play for violating Rule 20-7.

♜

An interesting twist on this issue of dropping on a paved cart path came up at the 2012 Players Championship. On the 18th hole of TPC Sawgrass, Kevin Na pushed his drive into the right rough and it ended up near a cart path in ground damaged by a maintenance cart's tire. He called a Ref, and the Ref deemed the tire track Ground Under Repair. There was very thick rough at the edges of the track, rough that many people might mindlessly drop in, but with what I'll call great presence of mind Mr. Na chose to take his relief by dropping on the paved cart path. He then pulled what looked like a fairway wood out, took a smooth swing and hit his ball off the path 241 yards to the green — and two-putted for a spectacular par.

ॐ ॐ ॐ

Rules:

Rule 6 - The Player
6-5. Ball

The responsibility for playing the proper ball rests with the player. Each player should put an identification mark on his ball.

Rule 12 - Searching for and Identifying Ball
12-2. Lifting Ball for Identification

The responsibility for playing the proper ball rests with the player. Each player should put an identification mark on his ball.

If a player believes that a ball at rest might be his, but he cannot identify it, the player may lift the ball for identification, without penalty. The right to lift a ball for identification is in addition to the actions permitted under Rule 12-1.

Before lifting the ball, the player must announce his intention to his opponent in match play or his marker or a fellow-competitor in stroke play and mark the position of the ball. He may then lift the ball and identify it, provided that he gives his opponent, marker or fellow-competitor an opportunity to observe the lifting and replacement. The ball must not be cleaned beyond the extent necessary for identification when lifted under Rule 12-2.

If the ball is the player's ball and he fails to comply with all or any part of this procedure, or he lifts his ball in order to identify it without having good reason to do so, he incurs a penalty of one stroke. If the lifted ball is the player's ball, he must replace it. If he fails to do so, he incurs the general penalty for a breach of Rule 12-2, but there is no additional penalty under this Rule.

Note: If the original lie of a ball to be replaced has been altered, see Rule 20-3b.

Rule 15 - Substituted Ball; Wrong Ball
15-3. Wrong Ball
a. Match Play

If a player makes a stroke at a wrong ball, he loses the hole.

If the wrong ball belongs to another player, its owner must place a ball on the spot from which the wrong ball was first played.

If the player and opponent exchange balls during the play of a hole, the first to make a stroke at a wrong ball loses the hole; when this cannot be determined, the hole must be played out with the balls exchanged.

✎ ✎ ✎

Exception: There is no penalty if a player makes a stroke at a wrong ball that is moving in water in a water hazard. Any strokes made at a wrong ball moving in water in a water hazard do not count in the player's score. The player must correct his mistake by playing the correct ball or by proceeding under the Rules.

(Placing and Replacing - see Rule 20-3)

b. Stroke Play

If a competitor makes a stroke or strokes at a wrong ball, he incurs a penalty of two strokes.

The competitor must correct his mistake by playing the correct ball or by proceeding under the Rules. If he fails to correct his mistake before making a stroke on the next teeing ground or, in the case of the last hole of the round, fails to declare his intention to correct his mistake before leaving the putting green, he is disqualified.

Strokes made by a competitor with a wrong ball do not count in his score. If the wrong ball belongs to another competitor, its owner must place a ball on the spot from which the wrong ball was first played.

Exception: There is no penalty if a competitor makes a stroke at a wrong ball that is moving in water in a water hazard. Any strokes made at a wrong ball moving in water in a water hazard do not count in the competitor's score.

(Placing and Replacing - see Rule 20-3)

☙ ☙ ☙

Become An Exterior Decorator

Under the topic of Player's Responsibilities, Rule 6-5 tells you that you should put an identifying mark on your ball. (In the "How to use the Rule Book" section at the beginning of the *Rules of Golf*, it tells you that "should" is a recommendation, not a commandment.) Rule 6-5 also tells you that the responsibility for playing the proper ball is yours. Further, in Rule 12-2, Lifting Ball for Identification, we are once again reminded that the player should put an identifying mark on his ball. Finally, Rule 15-3 tells you what to do if you end up hitting the wrong ball. (It's not pretty.)

It's clear that unless you are a devoted masochist, you should mark your ball so you can accurately identify it. What may not be clear is the fact that the way in which you mark it can make the difference between hitting your ball vs. hitting a wrong ball, and the difference between getting a drop vs. getting a Stroke and Distance penalty for a lost ball. Here are a couple of things a non-masochist might want to keep in mind when he sits down to decorate the exterior of his golf balls — as well as when he finds a ball he thinks may be his while he's playing

First, that Titleist 1 you just found in the rough may or may not be yours. (Believe it or not, other people play Titleist 1s as well.) If you didn't actually witness your ball coming to rest, it might be worthwhile to bend over and study the ball for your unique marking or even go through Rule 12-2's identification process and pick up the ball to make sure it's yours before you take a stroke at it. (Of course, having bold personal markings on the ball may make it easier to identify even without lifting it, but you may lift it if need be.)

Further, when you're deciding what mark to draw on your ball don't be so sure that you'll actually have the opportunity to turn your ball around in your hand and study it every time you attempt to identify it. What happens if you can see a ball, but you're not able to get to it in order to mark its position and lift it as you would if it was on the ground? I've had a tournament player get free relief for a ball that fell through a drainage grate because it was lying at the bottom of the deep hole in such a way that his meager mark happened to be turned upward. Had the ball been turned slightly in any direction, he would not have been able to identify the ball as his.

You might remember the 2013 WGC-Cadillac Championship in which Tiger Woods got his ball stuck in a tree at Doral's 17th hole. Tiger was able to identify his tee shot through use of binoculars, enabling him to take a drop beneath the tree with just a one-stroke Unplayable Ball penalty instead of having to suffer Stroke and Distance. In any situation like this, the bigger the marking you have on your ball, the more likely it is that you'll be able to identify it.

ꙮ

Admittedly, the tree and grate thing are odd occurrences. In these cases the very visible markings I'm advocating are more likely to help a pro who has a group of spectators pointing down into the grate or up at the tree than they are likely to help the rest of us. But on the other hand, PGA Tour pros don't have to suffer a stranger in a parallel fairway absentmindedly hitting their golf ball and absconding with it as do we players of public courses. And a PGA Tour pro playing a pristine course is less likely to accidentally find and hit someone else's abandoned ball by mistake.

A heavily-marked ball may not save you from any of these tragedies, but it just might. I think the cost of a little extra ink is worth it.

Rule:

Rule 14 - Striking the Ball
14-1. General
a. Fairly Striking the Ball
The ball must be fairly struck at with the head of the club and must not be pushed, scraped or spooned.

Decisions:

14-1a/1 Playing Stroke with Back of Clubhead
Q. May a player play a left-handed stroke with the back of the head of a right-handed club?
A. Yes. A player may play a stroke with any part of the clubhead, provided the ball is fairly struck at (Rule 14-1a) and the club conforms with Rule 4-1.

14-1a/3 Putting with Wrong End of Putter
Q. A player misses a short putt and hastily holes the ball with the wrong (handle) end of his putter. What is the ruling?
A. The player incurs a penalty of loss of hole in match play or two strokes in stroke play for a breach of Rule 14-1, which requires that the ball be struck at with the head of the club. In stroke play, the stroke with the wrong end of the putter counts, and, since the ball was holed, the player had completed play of the hole.

♜ ♜ ♜

Use More Club

No, I'm not going to tell you that you should hit your seven instead of your eight. I'm going to tell you that you are free to hit your ball with more parts of your clubhead than you might have considered. Rule 14 covers striking the ball, and 14-1a says we have to fairly strike the ball "with the head of the club." It doesn't say we have to use the face of the club, and Decision 14-1a/1 makes it perfectly clear that any part of the clubhead is fair game.

Some of us, and by some of us I mean me, are impressively lacking in skill at hitting opposite-handed. So if I turn my nine iron upside down to get the club's face on my ball with a left handed swing, the relatively small part of the face (the toe) that's left available to strike the ball is insufficiently wide for me to feel confident about making contact. On the other hand, using the entire width of the back side of the clubhead gives me the margin of error I feel I need. (The negative loft of the back of the club when held like that doesn't hurt me much when I'm only planning to punch a ball a modest distance with such a stroke anyway.)

♜

Another nice trick is to use the flat toe of your putter head to strike the ball from near the green if the ball or your backswing is impeded by thick rough on the fringe. A blade-style putter (instead of a mallet) is typically necessary to get any advantage from this, but if you carry one, instead of the large face of the putter getting stuck in the grass, the relatively thin toe slides effortlessly through it. This idea of using a smaller surface is the exact opposite of that which I just described regarding my opposite-handed shots, but for me at least the modest movement during the swing of a putt combined with using my normal right-handed stroke is all I need to get a decent shot at the ball. Don't get me wrong, I'm not so cruel as to suggest that you model your ball-striking after my game — I'm merely suggesting that you be aware of the fact that all parts of your clubhead are available to you in making a legal stroke. And I trust that sooner or later you'll find some occasion to make that work to your advantage.

Be sure you stick with striking the ball with a part of the clubhead though — Rule 14-1a demands that. Striking it with the grip, for instance, is a violation as is confirmed in Decision 14-1a/3.

🐞 🐞 🐞

Rule:

13-4. Ball in Hazard; Prohibited Actions

Except as provided in the Rules, before making a stroke at a ball that is in a hazard (whether a bunker or a water hazard) or that, having been lifted from a hazard, may be dropped or placed in the hazard, the player must not:

a. Test the condition of the hazard or any similar hazard;
b. Touch the ground in the hazard or water in the water hazard with his hand or a club; or
c. Touch or move a loose impediment lying in or touching the hazard.

Exceptions:

1. Provided nothing is done that constitutes testing the condition of the hazard or improves the lie of the ball, there is no penalty if the player (a) touches the ground or loose impediments in any hazard or water in a water hazard as a result of or to prevent falling, in removing an obstruction, in measuring or in marking the position of, retrieving, lifting, placing or replacing a ball under any Rule or (b) places his clubs in a hazard.
2. At any time, the player may smooth sand or soil in a hazard provided this is for the sole purpose of caring for the course and nothing is done to breach Rule 13-2 with respect to his next stroke. If a ball played from a hazard is outside the hazard after the stroke, the player may smooth sand or soil in the hazard without restriction.
3. If the player makes a stroke from a hazard and the ball comes to rest in another hazard, Rule 13-4a does not apply to any subsequent actions taken in the hazard from which the stroke was made.

Note: At any time, including at address or in the backward movement for the stroke, the player may touch, with a club or otherwise, any obstruction, any construction declared by the Committee to be an integral part of the course or any grass, bush, tree or other growing thing.

Decision:

13-4/30 Grounding Club on Bridge in Water Hazard

Q. A player's ball lies on a bridge over a water hazard within the margins of the hazard when extended upwards. May the player ground his club?

A. Yes. A bridge is an obstruction. In a hazard, the club may touch an obstruction at address or in the backward movement for the stroke - see Note under Rule 13-4. Touching the bridge prior to address is also permissible, since an obstruction in a water hazard is not "ground in the hazard."

This applies even if the bridge has been declared an integral part of the course.

꧁ ꧁ ꧁

Ground Your Club In A Hazard

Some people are particularly put off when they're not able to ground their club prior to a shot, and for them Rule 13-4 "Ball in Hazard; Prohibited Actions" takes an extra toll since part "b" precludes them from touching the ground with their club. Good news for these types, if your ball is on an Immovable Obstruction within the hazard, say resting on a bridge that goes across a Water Hazard, Decision 13-4/30 gives you carte blanche to ground your club on the Immovable Obstruction to your heart's delight. Small potatoes I guess, you're still stuck in a Water Hazard and unable to get free relief from an Immovable Obstruction because your ball is in a Water Hazard, but hey, it's something.

☙ ☙ ☙

Rule:

1-2. Exerting Influence on Movement of Ball or Altering Physical Conditions

A player must not (i) take an action with the intent to influence the movement of a ball in play or (ii) alter physical conditions with the intent of affecting the playing of a hole.

Exceptions:

1. An action expressly permitted or expressly prohibited by another Rule is subject to that other Rule, not Rule 1-2.
2. An action taken for the sole purpose of caring for the course is not a breach of Rule 1-2.

* Penalty for Breach of Rule 1-2:
Match play - Loss of hole; Stroke play - Two strokes.

* In the case of a serious breach of Rule 1-2, the Committee may impose a penalty of disqualification.

Note 1:   A player is deemed to have committed a serious breach of Rule 1-2 if the Committee considers that the action taken in breach of this Rule has allowed him or another player to gain a significant advantage or has placed another player, other than his partner, at a significant disadvantage.

Note 2:   In stroke play, except where a serious breach resulting in disqualification is involved, a player in breach of Rule 1-2 in relation to the movement of his own ball must play the ball from where it was stopped, or, if the ball was deflected, from where it came to rest. If the movement of a player's ball has been intentionally influenced by a fellow-competitor or other outside agency, Rule 1-4 applies to the player (see Note to Rule 19-1).

Decisions:

13-2/8.5 Player's Lie Affected by Sand from Partner's, Opponent's or Fellow-Competitor's Stroke from Bunker

Q. A's ball is on the apron between the green and a bunker. A's partner, opponent or fellow-competitor (B) plays from the bunker and deposits sand on and around A's ball. Is A entitled to any relief?

A. Yes. A is entitled to the lie and line of play he had when his ball came to rest. Accordingly, in equity (Rule 1-4), he is entitled to remove the sand deposited by B's stroke and lift his ball and clean it, without penalty.

13-2/8 Player's Lie or Line of Play Affected by Pitch-Mark Made by Partner's, Opponent's or Fellow-Competitor's Ball

Q. A player's lie, line of play or area of intended swing through the green is affected by a pitch-mark made by his partner's, his opponent's or a fellow-competitor's ball. Is the player entitled to repair the pitch-mark?

A. If the pitch-mark was there before the player's ball came to rest, he is not entitled to repair it if doing so would improve his lie, line of play, area of intended swing or other area covered by Rule 13-2.

If the pitch-mark was created after the player's ball came to rest, in equity (Rule 1-4), he may repair it. A player is entitled to the lie which his stroke gave him. (Revised)

13-2/8.7 Player's Area of Intended Stance Affected by Another Player's Stroke

Q. The balls of A and B lie near each other through the green. A plays and in doing so affects B's area of intended stance (e.g., by creating a divot hole). What is the ruling?

A. B may play the ball as it lies. In addition, if the original area of intended stance could be easily restored, in equity (Rule 1-4), the area of intended stance may be restored as nearly as possible, without penalty.

If the original area of intended stance could not be easily restored, in equity (Rule 1-4), the player may place his ball, without penalty, on the nearest spot within one club-length of the original lie that provides the most similar lie and area of intended stance to the original lie and area of intended stance. This spot must not be nearer the hole and must not be in a hazard.

20-3b/2 Lie in Bunker Changed by Another Player Taking His Stance

Q. In playing from a bunker, B, in taking his stance, pushed up a mound of sand behind A's ball, which had not been lifted. What is the ruling?

A. Since A's ball did not move when B took his stance, Rule 20-3b does not apply. In equity (Rule 1-4), A's original lie may be restored as nearly as possible by removing the mound of sand.

13-4/18 Partner's, Opponent's or Fellow-Competitor's Divot Comes to Rest Near Player's Ball in Bunker

Q. A player's partner, opponent or fellow-competitor plays a stroke from near a bunker and the divot comes to rest near the player's ball lying in the bunker. May the divot be removed?

A. A player is entitled to the lie which his stroke gave him. Accordingly, in equity (Rule 1-4), the divot may be removed without penalty.

The same would apply if the player's ball was lying in a water hazard.

Improve Your Lie/Line Of Play

Anyone who has read far enough in the *Rules of Golf* that they've reached Rule 1-2 knows that they can't alter physical conditions with the intent of affecting their play of a hole. At least they know they can't unless such an action is "expressly permitted" by another Rule — which of course is the subject of this segment. Most everyone knows that outside a hazard you may remove Loose Impediments that might impact your play prior to taking your shot, and you're always free to move Movable Obstructions, but here are noteworthy exceptions to the generality of Rule 1-2 that go well beyond those common acts.

A significant additional exception is hidden away in Decision 13-2/8.5, in which an important sentence emerges: A player "is entitled to the lie and line of play he had when his ball came to rest." That single sentence miraculously allows you to rewrite history: If your Partner, your Opponent or even an animate Outside Agency like a Fellow Competitor changes your lie or line of play after your ball comes to rest in a way that displeases you, you may change it back.

"Changing it back" is a rich area that includes the otherwise prohibited acts of repairing a pitch mark on the fringe you'd like to putt over, brushing away sand or loose soil deposited on the ground even though it's not on a putting green (and cleaning your ball if the sand or soil got deposited there by someone else), getting relief for your stance when another player makes a divot hole where you planned to stand, smoothing sand in a bunker that was altered by another player, and moving a grassy divot that just landed in front of your ball even though it's in a bunker. Decisions 13-2/8, 13-2/8.5, 13-2/8.7, 20-3b/2, 13-4/18 are the ones you'll want to wave in an adversary's face when you see he's about to challenge your seemingly unorthodox behavior.

Decisions:

13-4/37 Ball Played from Bunker Is Out of Bounds or Lost; Player Tests Condition of Bunker or Smoothes Footprints Before Dropping Another Ball in Bunker

Q. A player plays from a bunker and his ball comes to rest out of bounds or is lost. He smoothes his footprints in the bunker at the place where he must drop a ball under Rule 27-1 or, before dropping a ball under Rule 27-1, he takes a few practice swings touching the sand in the bunker. Is the player in breach of Rule 13-4?

A. No. The prohibitions in Rule 13-4 apply only when the player's ball is in the hazard or when it has been lifted from a hazard and may be dropped or placed in the hazard. In this case, the player's ball has been played from the hazard rather than lifted.

Furthermore, Exception 2 under Rule 13-4 allows a player, after playing his ball out of a hazard, to smooth sand or soil in the hazard without restriction. This right overrides any conflicting provisions in other Rules, including Rule 13-2.

23-1/6 Removal of Loose Impediments from Area in Which Ball to Be Dropped

Q. Through the green, is it permissible for a player to remove loose impediments from the area in which he is preparing to drop his ball?

A. Yes.

23-1/6.5 Removal of Loose Impediments from Spot Where Ball to Be Placed

Q. Through the green, a player taking relief under a Rule drops his ball and it rolls more than two club-lengths. He re-drops under Rule 20-2c, with the same result. He must now place the ball as near as possible to the spot where it first struck a part of the course when re-dropped - Rule 20-2c. Before he places the ball, may he remove loose impediments on or around the spot on which the ball is to be placed?

A. Yes.

If you've enjoyed all that, consider that there's sometimes an opportunity to legally improve your lie even if an Outside Agency isn't involved in altering it. At least, potentially improve your future lie via fixing things up before you drop. Decision 13-4/37 makes it clear that if you hit your ball Out of Bounds from a bunker (or lose it), before you take your drop as near as possible to that spot in the bunker from which you struck the ball you may smooth the sand without restriction. Similarly, before dropping a ball Through the Green, Decisions 23-1/6 and 23-1/6.5 give you permission to remove Loose Impediments that might end up interfering with your next shot — Loose Impediments that might be dangerous to move a few moments later if your ball ends up resting on or near them after your drop.

❦ ❦ ❦

Segment of Rule:

13-2. Improving Lie, Area of Intended Stance or Swing, or Line of Play

A player must not improve or allow to be improved:

- the position or lie of his ball

However, the player incurs no penalty if the action occurs:

- in creating or eliminating irregularities of surface within the teeing ground or in removing dew, frost or water from the teeing ground

Decisions:

13-2/2 Player Who Misses Tee Shot Presses Down Irregularities Before Next Stroke

Q. In playing a tee shot A misses the ball. Before playing his next stroke, A presses down turf behind the ball. Is this permissible, since the ball is in play?

A. Yes. Rule 13-2 permits eliminating irregularities of surface on the teeing ground, whether or not the ball is in play.

13-2/3 Breaking Off Grass Behind Ball on Teeing Ground

Q. Under Rule 13-2, it is permissible to eliminate irregularities of surface on the teeing ground. Is it also permissible to break off or pull out grass growing behind a ball on the teeing ground?

A. Yes.

⚑ ⚑ ⚑

Here's one last way for you to improve your lie: Rule 13-2 gives you total freedom in either "creating or eliminating irregularities of surface" within the teeing ground. As Decisions 13-2/2 and 13-2/3 confirm, that freedom includes breaking off grass, stomping down a slight mound or even digging a small hole behind your ball to effectively tee it up. Surprisingly, those aggressive actions are even allowed if your ball is already in play (as long as it's still in the two-club-length-deep teeing ground). I don't suppose you'd want to intentionally pop up a ball to have it stay in the teeing ground, but if you do, at least you can legally amuse yourself by improving your lie as long as you don't touch or move your ball.

⚑

All of this teeing ground alteration talk reminds me of watching England's superstar Laura Davies as she expertly slammed her club into the grass in order to create her very own brand of preferred "turf tee."

ত ত ত

Decisions:

17-3/3 Ball Strikes Flagstick Lying on Ground

Q. Generally, the player's ball must not strike the flagstick when removed from the hole (Rule 17-3). What is the ruling in the following situations:

  a. A player putts too strongly and his ball strikes the flagstick which has been removed by someone in his match or group and placed on the ground behind the hole.

  b. A player plays his second shot to the green and the ball strikes the flagstick, which had been blown down by the wind and was lying on the ground.

  c. A player, not believing he can reach the green which is occupied by the preceding match or group, plays his second shot at a par-5 hole and the ball rolls onto the green and strikes the flagstick which has been removed from the hole and placed on the ground by someone in the preceding match or group.

A. a. The player incurs a penalty of loss of hole in match play or two strokes in stroke play under Rule 17-3a;

b. & c. No penalty is incurred. Rule 17-3a is not applicable in either case. It applies only when the flagstick has been removed with the player's authority or prior knowledge by someone in the player's match or group.

23-1/10 Removal of Loose Impediments Affecting Player's Play

Q. A player with a downhill putt picks up loose impediments between his ball and the hole but leaves some behind the hole. An opponent or fellow-competitor removes loose impediments behind the hole that might have served as a backstop for the player's ball. What is the ruling?

A. In equity (Rule 1-4), the player is entitled, but not required, to replace the loose impediments. The opponent or fellow-competitor is permitted to remove the loose impediments by Rule 23-1, and accordingly he is not in breach of Rule 1-2 (see Exception 1 to Rule 1-2). However, if the opponent or fellow-competitor has refused to comply with a request from the player not to remove the loose impediments, the opponent loses the hole (see Decision 2/3) or the fellow-competitor is disqualified (Rule 3-4) for intentionally denying the player's right to have the loose impediments left in position.

The same principles apply to the removal of a movable obstruction in similar circumstances.

⚐ ⚐ ⚐

Use Things Lying On The Green As A Backstop

This won't happen often, but when it does your behavior might really surprise those playing with you.

On a windy day the group in front of you replaces the flagstick on the 18th hole carelessly, and a moment later the wind blows it over. Your approach to the green ends up on the fringe, and as it happens the flagstick is lying at an 8:00 angle to your chip shot, in a way that might slow it and feed the chip toward the hole if it contacts the pin. You have an impulse to walk over to the hole and replace the pin, but you stop and think, "That flagstick is simply a Moveable Obstruction. Maybe I like it right there where it is."

Yes, while you always have the right to move a Moveable Obstruction, in this case you don't have an obligation to move it. Decision 17-3/3 comes right out and tells us that since neither you nor anyone in your group put the pin there on the ground, you have the right to leave it where it was and chip right at it. So you chip, hit the pin lightly, and your ball rolls in the hole. Cool.

While a perverse situation like the above will be rare, more commonly you might decide to use Loose Impediments; perhaps leaves, acorns or twigs, in the exact same way if they're lying past or near the hole. In fact, if a person in your group innocently moves leaves out of the way to aid his shot coming the other way, you can put them back! Decision 23-1/10 details all that, and points out that the principle applies to replacing Movable Obstructions someone moved which you wanted left in place too. (Remember that flagstick we were talking about that was left lying on the green?)

❦ ❦ ❦

Rule:

Rule 28 - Ball Unplayable

The player may deem his ball unplayable at any place on the course, except when the ball is in a water hazard. The player is the sole judge as to whether his ball is unplayable.

If the player deems his ball to be unplayable, he must, under penalty of one stroke:

a. Proceed under the stroke and distance provision of Rule 27-1 by playing a ball as nearly as possible at the spot from which the original ball was last played (see Rule 20-5); or

b. Drop a ball behind the point where the ball lay, keeping that point directly between the hole and the spot on which the ball is dropped, with no limit to how far behind that point the ball may be dropped; or

c. Drop a ball within two club-lengths of the spot where the ball lay, but not nearer the hole.

If the unplayable ball is in a bunker, the player may proceed under Clause a, b or c. If he elects to proceed under Clause b or c, a ball must be dropped in the bunker.

When proceeding under this Rule, the player may lift and clean his ball or substitute a ball.

Penalty for Breach of Rule:
Match play - Loss of hole; Stroke play - Two strokes.

Segment of Rule:

20-2. Dropping and Re-Dropping
c. When to Re-Drop

A dropped ball must be re-dropped, without penalty, if it:

v. rolls to and comes to rest in a position where there is interference by the condition from which relief was taken under Rule 24-2b (immovable obstruction), Rule 25-1 (abnormal ground conditions), Rule 25-3 (wrong putting green) or a Local Rule (Rule 33-8a), or rolls back into the pitch-mark from which it was lifted under Rule 25-2 (embedded ball);

Decisions:

28/3 Ball Dropped Under Unplayable Ball Rule Comes to Rest in Original Position or Another Position at Which Ball Is Unplayable

Q. A player deemed his ball unplayable and, under Rule 28c, dropped his ball within two club-lengths of the spot where it lay. The ball came to rest in the original position or another position at which the ball was unplayable. What is the ruling?

A. The ball was in play when it was dropped - Rule 20-4. Thus, if the ball came to rest in the original position, the player must again invoke the unplayable ball Rule, incurring an additional penalty stroke, unless he decides to play the ball as it lies. The same applies if the ball came to rest in another position at which it was unplayable, assuming that the ball did not roll into a position covered by Rule 20-2c, in which case re-dropping without penalty would be required.

☙ ☙ ☙

28/5 Regression Under Unplayable Ball Rule

Q. A player plays a stroke from Point A to Point B. Point B is in an area from which it is very difficult to extricate the ball. The player considers deeming the ball unplayable but this would result in a stroke-and-distance penalty (Rule 28a). Dropping behind under Rule 28b is impossible due to a boundary fence and dropping within two club-lengths under Rule 28c is not feasible because it would require a considerable number of such drops to escape the area. The player plays from Point B and moves the ball a few feet to Point C, where the ball is clearly unplayable. Under Rule 28a, may the player:
   a. deem the ball unplayable at Point C and drop a ball under penalty of one stroke at Point B, and then
   b. deem the ball unplayable at Point B and drop a ball, under an additional penalty of one stroke, at Point A?

A. No. Under Rule 28a, the player would be entitled to drop a ball only at the place from which he played his last stroke (Point B).
   In the circumstances, the player's only alternative is to invoke Rule 28c a sufficient number of times (starting at Point C and dropping the ball sideways within two club-lengths each time) to get the ball into a playable position.

28/7 Player Misses Ball and Deems It Unplayable

Q. A player's tee shot comes to rest in tree roots. He makes a stroke, fails to move the ball and then deems the ball unplayable. May the player return to the tee, playing 4, under Rule 28a?

A. No. Rule 28a permits the player to play "a ball ... at the spot from which the original ball was last played." The original ball was last played from the tree roots, not the tee.

28/6.5 Player Deems Ball Unplayable a Second Time and Wishes to Proceed Under Stroke and Distance After Dropping a Ball Under Other Unplayable Option

Q. A player plays a stroke from Point A to Point B. The player deems his ball unplayable and proceeds under either Rule 28b or 28c. After dropping under penalty of one stroke, the ball comes to rest at Point C. The player deems his ball unplayable for a second time and wishes to proceed under Rule 28a, playing from Point A. Is this permissible?

A. Yes. The player may play from Point A because he did not make a stroke at the ball from either Point B or Point C. Point A was the spot from which the original ball was last played. The player would incur a total of two penalty strokes.

Remember To Avoid Déjà Vu

Rule 28, Ball Unplayable, can be a godsend, I'm sure you've used it to your advantage on many occasions. But the unwary might not recognize that there are a couple of significant dangers that arise in its employ.

An appealing part of the Rule is the fact that as long as your ball is outside of a Water Hazard, you're the boss in regard to whether it's "unplayable" or not. You say it is? It is. But there's a corollary to this freedom. Since there is no Rules-based description of the condition from which you might choose to take relief (as there is for an Abnormal Ground Condition or an Immovable Obstruction), it follows that if your dropped ball bounces back into the exact same situation that caused you to want relief in the first place you don't get a free re-drop. No sir, if you look carefully at Rule 20-2c (v), which directs you to re-drop if your ball ends up with continued interference from an Abnormal Ground Condition, Immovable Obstruction or Wrong Putting Green, you'll note that Unplayable Ball is conspicuously absent. As horrific as it might sound, after taking a drop for an Unplayable Ball you might end up stuck in the exact same mess — only your score is now one stroke higher for the privilege of watching the horror unfold. Your choices? Play it, or take yet another penalty drop.

If that repetitive trauma isn't chilling enough, consider this: Unplayable Ball relief comes in three flavors — Stroke and Distance, within two club-lengths, and dropping on an extension of a line from the pin to behind the unplayable lie itself. Let's say you are up against a boundary fence which restricts your backswing. You think about calling the ball unplayable, but instead decide to take a swipe at it — but the awkward swing causes you to miss the ball entirely. Now, déjà vu-like, you are faced with the exact same shot. Only now, since the spot from which your ball was "last played" (via your whiff) is the very spot it's still on, you've effectively given up the Stroke and Distance option you previously had, and now the only Unplayable Ball relief options you might be able to still consider are the two club-lengths and extension of the imaginary line. The extension of the imaginary line is void since that drop would leave you Out of Bounds, so the single available option is two club-lengths from the unplayable spot no closer to the hole. Let's just hope that this area doesn't slope back down toward the fence. If it does, you might be whiffing or dropping there for a long time.

If all this sounds too implausibly cruel to be true, read Decisions 28/3, 28/5 and 28/7. Or maybe I should say, "Read them and weep." Decision 28/6.5 provides a ray of hope in some cases, but the bottom line on all of this is that you really should follow Sergeant Phil Esterhaus's morning admonition to his patrol officers in the *Hill Street Blues* TV police drama: "Hey, let's be careful out there."

❦❦❦

Rule:

27-1. Stroke and Distance; Ball Out of Bounds; Ball Not Found Within Five Minutes

a. Proceeding Under Stroke and Distance

At any time, a player may, under penalty of one stroke, play a ball as nearly as possible at the spot from which the original ball was last played (see Rule 20-5), i.e., proceed under penalty of stroke and distance.

Except as otherwise provided in the Rules, if a player makes a stroke at a ball from the spot at which the original ball was last played, he is deemed to have proceeded under penalty of stroke and distance.

Enjoy A Good Stroke And Distance Penalty Every Now And Then

Certainly, the harshness of a Stroke and Distance penalty is generally something you want to avoid. But Stroke and Distance isn't always a punishment, sometimes it's a privilege. You might recall that's the way Tiger Woods saw it on Augusta National's 13th hole during the first round of the 2005 Masters.

Tiger was on the par five 13th green in two. Unfortunately, his downhill putt gathered too much speed and made its way past the hole to the front of the green, then went a touch further and tumbled into Rae's Creek. Tiger would either have to deal with the hazard or, as Rule 27-1 permits at any time, impose a Stroke and Distance penalty upon himself. Tiger was wise to take the Stroke and Distance option — he replaced the ball on the green at the cost of a penalty stroke and two putted for his bogey. Of course we don't know what would have ended up happening if he instead decided to take a drop from the hazard, but we do know that Tiger ended up winning in a playoff that year with no strokes to spare. I'd say that cool headedness and Stroke and Distance came to his rescue.

Any time you hit into a tough place and don't have to give up too much distance for the "distance" part of the Stroke and Distance penalty, you certainly want to give this option some consideration. Toe one 90 degrees off the first tee into the woods next weekend? Would you rather be lying two back on the teeing ground with your ball sitting back on a peg, or behind some brush lying one and hoping to punch out back toward the tee?

Rule:

Rule 18 - Ball at Rest Moved
18-1. By Outside Agency
If a ball at rest is moved by an outside agency, there is no penalty and the ball must be replaced.

Note: It is a question of fact whether a ball has been moved by an outside agency. In order to apply this Rule, it must be known or virtually certain that an outside agency has moved the ball. In the absence of such knowledge or certainty, the player must play the ball as it lies or, if the ball is not found, proceed under Rule 27-1.

(Player's ball at rest moved by another ball - see Rule 18-5)

Definition:

Outside Agency
In match play, an "outside agency" is any agency other than either the player's or opponent's side, any caddie of either side, any ball played by either side at the hole being played or any equipment of either side.

In stroke play, an outside agency is any agency other than the competitor's side, any caddie of the side, any ball played by the side at the hole being played or any equipment of the side.

An outside agency includes a referee, a marker, an observer and a forecaddie. Neither wind nor water is an outside agency.

Decisions:

18-1/12 Ball Replaced and at Rest Is Thereafter Moved by Wind

Q. A player replaces his ball on the putting green and the ball is at rest. Before the player addresses the ball, a sudden gust of wind blows the ball farther from the hole. The player plays the ball from its new position. Is that correct?

A. Yes. Wind is not an outside agency - see Definition of "Outside Agency." Accordingly, Rule 18-1 does not apply.

20-3d/1 Placed Ball Rolls into Hole

Q. A replaces his ball on the putting green three feet from the hole. Without doing anything to cause the ball to move, it rolls into the hole. Should the ball be replaced or is A deemed to have holed out with his previous stroke?

A. The answer depends on whether the ball, when replaced, came to rest on the spot on which it was placed before it started rolling. If it did, A is deemed to have holed out with his previous stroke. If not, A is required to replace the ball (Rule 20-3d). However, if the ball had been overhanging the hole when it was lifted, the provisions of Rule 16-2 would override those of Rule 20-3d. (Revised)

🍐 🍐 🍐

20-4/1 Ball Replaced on Putting Green But Ball-Marker Not Removed; Ball Then Moves

Q. A player replaces his ball on the putting green but does not remove his ball-marker. Subsequently the wind moves his ball to a new position. What is the ruling?

A. Under Rule 20-4, a ball is in play when it is replaced, whether or not the object used to mark its position has been removed. Consequently the ball must be played from the new position - see Decision 18-1/12.

Tilt Things To Your Advantage

You landed your ball on the green. It's in play. While Rule 18-1 tells us that a ball at rest must be replaced if it's moved by an Outside Agency, the definition of Outside Agency tells us that neither wind nor water are Outside Agencies — so if a breeze moves your ball it has to be played from its new location. (Decision 18-1/12 confirms that this is true even after your ball has been marked and replaced.) That new location might just be a better one.

Reportedly, Jack Nicklaus had a strategy for dealing with such situations. If practical, he'd leave the ball down on a sharply sloping green if it was above the hole, and be sure to mark and lift it if he was below the hole. He was just fine with the prospect of having to play the ball from its new location closer to the hole if it happened to roll towards it off a downslope, and disinclined to have to play from further away as would likely be the case if his ball was blown from its uphill lie prior to the wind getting it rolling. I encourage you to follow Jack's lead in this matter, let the tilt of the green guide you.

As a special treat, note that Decision 20-3d/1 tells us that a ball that was placed on the putting green, came to rest, and was subsequently blown into the hole by the wind is deemed to have been holed on the previous stroke. Pretty nice. By the way, don't forget that Decision 20-4/1 says that if your replaced ball is moved by the wind it has to be played from its new position even if the ball blew away while your ball marker was still sitting there. If you want to protect your ball from moving on the green, you have to lift it!

Definition:

Casual Water

"Casual water" is any temporary accumulation of water on the course that is not in a water hazard and is visible before or after the player takes his stance. Snow and natural ice, other than frost, are either casual water or loose impediments, at the option of the player. Manufactured ice is an obstruction. Dew and frost are not casual water.

A ball is in casual water when it lies in or any part of it touches the casual water.

Decisions:

23/14 Loose Impediments Used to Surface Road

Q. A player hits his ball onto a gravel-covered road. Even though he is entitled to relief from this obstruction, he prefers to play the ball from the road. May he remove gravel that might interfere with his stroke?

A. Yes. Gravel is a loose impediment and a player may remove loose impediments under Rule 23-1. This right is not canceled by the fact that, when a road is covered with gravel, it becomes an artificially-surfaced road and thus an immovable obstruction. The same principle applies to roads or paths constructed with stone, crushed shell, wood chips or the like.

25/6 Status of Saliva

Q. What is the status of saliva?

A. In equity (Rule 1-4), saliva may be treated as either an abnormal ground condition (Rule 25-1) or a loose impediment (Rule 23-1), at the option of the player.

⚐ ⚐ ⚐

See Things Your Way

There are a number of instances in the Rules where you get your druthers. So by all means, go ahead — but choose wisely.

The Definition of Casual Water tells us that we may view snow and natural ice (though not frost) as being either Casual Water or a Loose Impediment, at our option. The difference can be significant — for one thing the relief options are distinct. In the case of Casual Water you move your ball, with Loose Impediments you move the impediments. Where would you rather play from? Perhaps even more important is that if you're Through the Green, moving a Loose Impediment puts you at risk for being penalized for accidentally moving your ball when you move the impediment. That's not an issue when you lift and drop if you instead decide it's Casual Water from which you're taking relief.

⚐

Similarly, Decision 23/14 informs us that when a ball rests on a path artificially surfaced with gravel, crushed shell, wood chips or the like we have the option of either playing the ball from where it lies after moving these Loose Impediments (being careful not to accidentally move our ball), or alternately we can lift our ball and take complete free relief from the Immovable Obstruction that the gravel-covered path in its entirety represents.

⚐

Here's a less than genteel topic the normally courtly Rules stoop to address — according to Decision 25/6 you may choose to deem spit as either an Abnormal Ground Condition or a Loose Impediment. Either way you have a gross situation on your hands, but hey, at least relief is afforded — two different forms of relief at that. And the Abnormal Ground Condition choice doesn't penalize you if you accidentally move your ball that was sitting on the fringe up against that big tobacco-laden loogie the guy in the group in front of you rudely deposited. The Abnormal Ground Condition choice also allows you to clean your ball. Good times!

Decisions:

25/3 Pitch-Mark Filled with Casual Water

Q. A player's ball plugged deeply in short rough. No casual water was visible on the surface, but the pitch-mark in which the ball came to rest was filled with water. Was the player's ball in casual water?

A. Yes.

25-2/4 Ball Embedded in Ground Under Repair in Closely-Mown Area

Q. A player's ball is embedded in ground under repair in a closely-mown area through the green. May the player drop the ball within the ground under repair under Rule 25-2 (Embedded Ball) and then elect whether to play the ball as it lies or take relief from the ground under repair under Rule 25-1b?

A. Yes.

Rules:

Rule 10 - Order of Play
10-1. Match Play
c. Playing Out of Turn

If a player plays when his opponent should have played, there is no penalty, but the opponent may immediately require the player to cancel the stroke so made and, in correct order, play a ball as nearly as possible at the spot from which the original ball was last played (see Rule 20-5).

Rule 19 - Ball in Motion Deflected or Stopped
19-3. By Opponent, Caddie or Equipment in Match Play

If a player's ball is accidentally deflected or stopped by an opponent, his caddie or his equipment, there is no penalty. The player may, before another stroke is made by either side, cancel the stroke and play a ball, without penalty, as nearly as possible at the spot from which the original ball was last played (Rule 20-5) or he may play the ball as it lies. However, if the player elects not to cancel the stroke and the ball has come to rest in or on the opponent's or his caddie's clothes or equipment, the ball must through the green or in a hazard be dropped, or on the putting green be placed, as near as possible to the spot directly under the place where the ball came to rest in or on the article, but not nearer the hole.

Exception: Ball striking person attending or holding up flagstick or anything carried by him - see Rule 17-3b.

(Ball purposely deflected or stopped by opponent or caddie - see Rule 1-2)

An Embedded Ball might be in a pitch mark that, when the ball is lifted, shows visible water in it. If it's outside a hazard in a closely mown area (or in deeper grass if the Local Rule allowing relief from an Embedded Ball Through the Green is in effect), Decision 25/3 shows that you've once again got a choice as to which condition you'd like to take relief from — and consequently you'll have a choice as to where you'll be allowed to drop. In some cases that could be the difference between having to drop in the rough and getting to drop in the fairway.

Now let's say there's an Embedded Ball in a fairway in an area marked as Ground Under Repair. Decision 25-2/4 informs us that we may choose to take relief from either the Embedded Ball or Ground Under Repair condition — and after achieving relief from the condition we chose, still maintain the option of taking relief from the other condition if it still challenges our happiness.

The same thing occurs if your lie is interfered with by two independent Immovable Obstructions at the same time — maybe a paved cart path a few feet away from a building. Consider where you will get to drop from each Obstruction before deciding which Obstruction from which to first choose relief. Sometimes in these "you pick it" multiple interference situations the relief you might be afforded by the subsequent Obstruction will put you in a place that's dramatically different from where a single relief drop would land you, so by all means think things through.

ꠛ

In Match Play, there are a couple of big-deal "do over" options that are thrown your way, each resolved solely by how you see things benefitting you. If your Opponent plays out of turn either from the tee or while playing the hole, Rule 10-1c allows you the luxury of letting the infraction stand or immediately cancelling his shot. And it's not only your Opponent's shot that on occasion you might have the right to cancel: If a ball you hit gets deflected or stopped by your Opponent, his caddie or his equipment, Rule 19-3 says it's totally up to you whether you'd like to play it as it lies or replay the shot — as long as you take action before another stroke is made by either side.

ꝥ ꝥ ꝥ

Segments of Rules:

33-1. Conditions; Waiving Rule

The Committee has no power to waive a Rule of Golf.

33-8. Local Rules

a. Policy

The Committee may establish Local Rules for local abnormal conditions if they are consistent with the policy set forth in Appendix I.

b. Waiving or Modifying a Rule

A Rule of Golf must not be waived by a Local Rule. However, if a Committee considers that local abnormal conditions interfere with the proper playing of the game to the extent that it is necessary to make a Local Rule that modifies the Rules of Golf, the Local Rule must be authorized by the USGA.

1-3. Agreement to Waive Rules

Players must not agree to exclude the operation of any Rule or to waive any penalty incurred.
Penalty for Breach of Rule 1-3:

Match play - Disqualification of both sides; Stroke play - Disqualification of competitors concerned.
(Agreeing to play out of turn in stroke play - see Rule 10-2c)

34-1. Claims and Penalties

a. Match Play

If a claim is lodged with the Committee under Rule 2-5, a decision should be given as soon as possible so that the state of the match may, if necessary, be adjusted. If a claim is not made in accordance with Rule 2-5, it must not be considered by the Committee.
There is no time limit on applying the disqualification penalty for a breach of Rule 1-3.

b. Stroke Play

In stroke play, a penalty must not be rescinded, modified or imposed after the competition has closed. A competition is closed when the result has been officially announced or, in stroke play qualifying followed by match play, when the player has teed off in his first match.

Exceptions: A penalty of disqualification must be imposed after the competition has closed if a competitor:
    i. was in breach of Rule 1-3 (Agreement to Waive Rules);

❦ ❦ ❦

Decision:

33-7/9 Competitor Who Knows Player Has Breached Rules Does Not Inform Player or Committee in Timely Manner

The responsibility for knowing the Rules lies with all players. In stroke play, the player and his marker have an explicit responsibility for the correctness of the player's score card.

There may, however, be exceptional individual cases where, in order to protect the interests of every other player in the competition, it would be reasonable to expect a fellow-competitor or another competitor to bring to light a player's breach of the Rules by notifying the player, his marker or the Committee.

In such exceptional circumstances, it would be appropriate for the Committee to impose a penalty of disqualification under Rule 33-7 on a fellow-competitor or another competitor if it becomes apparent that he has failed to advise the player, his marker or the Committee of a Rules breach with the clear intention of allowing that player to return an incorrect score.

Segment of Rule:

Rule 2 - Match Play
2-5. Doubt as to Procedure; Disputes and Claims

In match play, if a doubt or dispute arises between the players, a player may make a claim. If no duly authorized representative of the Committee is available within a reasonable time, the players must continue the match without delay. The Committee may consider a claim only if it has been made in a timely manner and if the player making the claim has notified his opponent at the time (i) that he is making a claim or wants a ruling and (ii) of the facts upon which the claim or ruling is to be based.

A claim is considered to have been made in a timely manner if, upon discovery of circumstances giving rise to a claim, the player makes his claim (i) before any player in the match plays from the next teeing ground, or (ii) in the case of the last hole of the match, before all players in the match leave the putting green, or (iii) when the circumstances giving rise to the claim are discovered after all the players in the match have left the putting green of the final hole, before the result of the match has been officially announced.

Note 1: A player may disregard a breach of the Rules by his opponent provided there is no agreement by the sides to waive a Rule (Rule 1-3).

Be Nice

The Rules couldn't be more serious about being taken seriously. Rule 33-1 tells us that not even the Committee may waive a Rule. Rule 33-8 tells us that the Committee is even prevented from enacting a Local Rule that isn't "consistent with the policy" described in Appendix I unless special permission is granted by the USGA (or R&A if you happen to be reading their version of the Rule book). And Rule 1-3 tells us that if players agree to waive a Rule they are disqualified. Perhaps even more emphatic, like the crime of murder, the crime of waiving a Rule of Golf has no statute of limitations... Rule 34-1 tells us in no uncertain terms that there is no time limit on applying this particular disqualification penalty — even after the competition has closed.

Remarkably, this gets even more dramatic. Decision 33-7/9 warns that in Stroke Play, if we know a player has breached a Rule and don't bring this to the attention of the player, his Marker or the Committee, we might be disqualified ourselves if it was clear that we had the intention of allowing the player to return an incorrect score. If there's one thing the Rules care about, it's the Rules!

So where's an opportunity to "be nice?" One is kind of hidden in Note 1 of Match Play Rule 2-5, and it's decidedly for Match Play only: "A player may disregard a breach of the Rules by his opponent provided there is no agreement by the sides to waive a Rule (Rule 1-3)." Given the severity of the penalty for waiving a Rule, please be clear on the difference between disregarding a breach of a Rule and agreeing to waive it. "Agreeing" to waive a Rule requires both sides to know that they are waiving a Rule, but disregarding a violation is a single-sided behavior (as long as you don't bring your intention to disregard a Rule to your Opponent's attention). Silence is golden!

Let's say you're playing a Match against me, and you're ignorant of the requirement in Rule 8-1b that you may not ask me for advice. In violation of this Rule, after I strike my tee shot on a par three and before you strike yours, you ask me what club I used. I have the right to claim the hole based on the associated penalty in Rule 8-1, but if for whatever reason I wish to forgive your mistake I also have the right to avoid pointing it out. I may stay silent on the issue, and move on with the hole. As long as I don't actually point your violation out to you, we may legally continue to play the hole to its conclusion.

⚑ ⚑ ⚑

To put a finer point on this, in the depths of Rule 2-5 we can see that if it's my intention to be nice to you and avoid claiming the hole on the basis of your error, I must stay silent about my largess until one of us tees off on the next hole (or we both leave the 18th green). After that I may alert you to the fact that I gave you a break, but if I tell you before one of us tees off on the next hole we'd both be stuck with either having to accept your loss of hole penalty, or "stuck" with our both being disqualified from the entire Match since we otherwise violated Rule 1-3's demand that we not agree to waive a penalty.

By all means, be nice in Match Play if you wish. It adds richness to our game. But be careful about the timing!

❦ ❦ ❦

Segment of a Rule:

Rule 18 - Ball at Rest Moved

18-1. By Outside Agency

If a ball at rest is moved by an outside agency, there is no penalty and the ball must be replaced.

18-2. By Player, Partner, Caddie or Equipment

Except as permitted by the Rules, when a player's ball is in play, if

i.   the player, his partner or either of their caddies:
  - lifts or moves the ball,
  - touches it purposely (except with a club in the act of addressing the ball), or
  - causes the ball to move, or

ii. the equipment of the player or his partner causes the ball to move, the player incurs a penalty of one stroke.

18-3. By Opponent, Caddie or Equipment in Match Play

a.   During Search

If, during search for a player's ball, an opponent, his caddie or his equipment, moves the ball, touches it or causes it to move, there is no penalty. If the ball is moved, it must be replaced.

Here's another way to be nice that applies equally to both Stroke Play and Match Play: Help another player find his ball. That's obviously a nice thing to do for someone — but did you know that it's also a circumstance in which you are in a unique position to help in a way that's significantly more effective than the player can muster for himself?

While there are some sand/water/Obstruction/Ground Under Repair exceptions to note if you read the entirety of Rule 12 and Rule 18-2, generally speaking if a player accidentally moves his ball while he searches for it he incurs a penalty stroke via Rule 18-2 and is obligated to replace his ball. That amounts to a pretty big inhibition for a guy desperately searching in tall grass with the clock running down on his five minute search period.

Fortunately, the Rules intercede in an interesting way that not only provides you with the opportunity to be gracious to another player, but also protects you from penalty while you're being gracious. In Stroke Play you are technically an Outside Agency in relationship to someone with whom you are grouped (in addition to being their Fellow Competitor). As you can see reading Rule 18-1, there's no penalty to anyone if you (or your caddie) accidentally move another player's ball. In Match Play, if you or your caddie move your Opponent's ball while helping him search for it, you and he are also exonerated from penalty as described in Rule 18-3.

If you'd like (and the Rules pretty much encourage you) you're free to stomp around in the grass or spread it with your hands or probe through leaves with your club — oblivious to whether you accidentally smack your Fellow Competitor's or Opponent's ball in the process. In contrast, the player you're helping must make absolutely sure he doesn't move his ball while he conducts the same search.

It's a friendly, charitable thing to do. And, as they say, it might well end up being a case of "bread upon the waters."

Nice.

♜ ♜ ♜

Show Your Spirit

Beyond choosing to overlook an Opponent's innocent mistake or help a player find his ball there's another, broader Rules-inspired opportunity to "be nice" that I'd like to focus on as I end this chapter, and as I near the end of this book. I referenced it in the Introduction and, at least for me, it's the single best thing about golf.

The very first section of the Rules holds the Etiquette section. It's well worth reading for any number of reasons, but I think most importantly because it is there where we find the description of "The Spirit of the Game."

The Spirit of the Game

Golf is played, for the most part, without the supervision of a referee or umpire. The game relies on the integrity of the individual to show consideration for other players and to abide by the Rules. All players should conduct themselves in a disciplined manner, demonstrating courtesy and sportsmanship at all times, irrespective of how competitive they may be. This is the spirit of the game of golf.

Those sentences define the spiritual basis of golf, separating it from other sports and other perspectives on what a "competition" should aspire to. We who play golf are not encouraged to mislead a Ref, we are not encouraged to hide our errors from other players; instead we are straightforwardly asked to play openly and fairly.

I don't mind the baseball infielder pretending that he tagged the runner sliding into second when he knows he missed. I'm not offended by the basketball player feigning falling backwards, hoping the Ref will call a charging foul on his opponent moving aggressively toward the basket. This type of subtle subterfuge is an accepted part of many sports, and it's certainly in that sense "fair" in the context of those sports. But while I easily accept those behaviors, in contrast I absolutely love the fact that golf just flat-out asks us to be honest.

I absolutely love it.

⚑ ⚑ ⚑

VI. HOW TO GET MORE DEEPLY INVOLVED WITH THE RULES

Once You've Fallen In Love You'll Want To Spend More Time Together

I hope by now I've moved you. Maybe you feel more connected to the Rules of Golf than you had in the past. But beyond playing and competing, where else can you go with that feeling? Let me share my own adventure and see if anything resonates for you.

Although I was devoted to the Rules ever since I was a kid, up until about ten years ago my relationship with them was just for my own satisfaction. I didn't play in many formal competitions so this strong connection was principally "in my head." But something significant happened in 2006: The Ruling Bodies decided that it would now be legal to use Distance Measuring Devices as long as a Course Committee or Competition Committee enacted the newly approved Local Rule regarding DMDs.

Lasers had been around for a while, and though I didn't own one due to their being illegal, I very much wanted them to be permitted. The minute they were I went out and bought one. Being fastidious about the Rules I dutifully checked to see if each course I was playing had the DMD Local Rule in place. I was dismayed to discover how hard it was to find out. In my quest I took the trouble to carefully read many courses' scorecards to see if the new Local Rule was mentioned. (It wasn't.) I tried complaining about this omission to my golf buddies to see if that was satisfying. (It wasn't.)

Then one day it occurred to me, "Instead of complaining, why don't you try to fix it?" I decided to write to Paul Grillo, the Executive Director of Sterling Farms Golf Course (my local muni) and offer my help. I was a bit apprehensive that he was a very busy guy who might not have time to be bothered with such a detail, but I was delighted to discover that I was wrong. I offered to re-write the back of the scorecard, and ended up doing so with Paul's encouragement. He got some other interested parties to review and approve my suggested changes, and then adjusted the scorecards the next time they were printed.

I hope it doesn't sound too goofy, but that was a pretty big deal for me.

The next step in my evolution started when I was at a party talking to my neighbor's cousin, Walter Janeczko, a golf pro at nearby Knollwood Country Club. Naturally I drove the conversation to quirky Rules issues, and given my obvious (obsessive?) interest he ended up suggesting that I get in touch with his friend, the Executive Director of the Westchester Golf Association, in hopes of my becoming a volunteer Rules official. The WGA has been around since 1916, and its membership includes clubs as prestigious as Winged Foot, Westchester Country Club and the Stanwich Club, so I was intimidated — but my interest overwhelmed my apprehension and I set up a meeting.

I was invited to volunteer, and that launched a significant expansion of my relationship with the Rules. There's a big difference between being devoted to playing by the Rules and making rulings regarding someone else's play. (Notably, you always know your own intentions, and most always know what actions you have taken — but it's not so easy to "see into the soul" of another player.)

The WGA does a very nice job of orienting its volunteers though, and its Executive Director, Bob Thomas, and Tournament Director, Mike Zamalkany, were instrumental in helping me find my way. There are Rules seminars conducted for the volunteers by some excellent and highly credentialed teachers, and perhaps even more important there's a radio on your hip through which you can confer with other officials in real time when you're out there on your own. It didn't take long to get comfortable with the responsibility.

One particularly satisfying aspect of getting my relationship with the Rules out of my own head and into the real world was that I was able to confirm that the knowledge I collected by studying the written word fit well with the actual practices of the real-world Refs with whom I was now rubbing shoulders. I was now confident that my academic understanding of the Rules was the real deal.

☙

The next thing I decided to do was to get involved with the Men's Club at the local muni I referred to earlier. My Rules interest and expertise were welcomed with open arms. Nowadays I chair the Sterling Farms Men's Club's Rules Committee, compete in our tournaments most every weekend during the season, regularly correspond with members regarding their Rules questions, and enjoy working with both the Club and the course itself in defining which Local Rules we'll adopt as well as the course's setup regarding Ground Under Repair, Dropping Zones, hazard lines and the like.

I also host an annual Rules Seminar for the Club, where our members collect to drink beer, muse about Rules issues particular to our course, and get more of their Rules questions answered. We've recently expanded that night to include discussion on the USGA's Handicap Rules, and now our Handicap Chairman and my new friend Mitchell Schepps participates as well. (I should add that we invite the course's Women's Club members to participate too, and both clubs use the night as an opportunity to get prospective members to join our two groups.)

⚑

Some time after joining the Men's Club I signed up for the PGA/USGA three and a half day Rules of Golf Workshop discussed earlier. It was a truly interesting, rewarding and exhausting experience where I had the opportunity to take the (grueling) test at the end of the course. Now I had the definitive yardstick to measure my expertise, and thankfully that whole effort proved to be a success: I managed to achieve the highest level, the one necessary to officiate in a U.S. Open. You can probably guess by now that was a major thrill for me.

With that credential in tow, I soon volunteered to also become a Rules official for the Metropolitan Golf Association and became a member of its Rules & Competitions Committee. Founded in 1897, the MGA is one of the largest and oldest regional golf associations in the country and is responsible for everything from rating courses and providing handicap services to running its own tournaments and conducting USGA qualifying rounds — including Local and Sectional qualifying rounds for the U.S. Open itself.

The rigor and precision that the MGA and its Executive Director, Brian Mahoney, apply to officiating and the organization's close association with the USGA have provided me with yet another enriching opportunity to involve myself with like-minded people and further express my love for this game.

⚑

Oh, yeah, one more thing. I wrote a book.

⚐ ⚐ ⚐

So, where else might you go to explore your affection for the Rules of Golf? I don't know, I'm not done searching myself, and I'm sure there are other paths to take.

If you're interested in sharing any of your experiences with me (or you simply want to comment about this book) please shoot me an email at Howard.Meditz@gmail.com. I'd enjoy hearing from you.